OP

35.00

AMERICAN CUT GLASS

For The Discriminating Collector

Punch bowl, 14" in diameter, and matching punch cups by Dorflinger in their Middlesex pattern. Silver ladle of same design is stamped "Dorflinger."

A. Cookie jar, height including cover 8¼" by Schotten Glass Co. of Brooklyn, N.Y.; B. Covered apothecary jar, 15" over-all height, clear knob with controlled bubbles (Pairpoint); C. Vase by Dorflinger, 10½" tall, ornate sterling top with gold wash.

AMERICAN
CUT GLASS

For The Discriminating Collector

J. MICHAEL PEARSON

and

DOROTHY T. PEARSON

VANTAGE PRESS NEW YORK WASHINGTON HOLLYWOOD

Dedicated to the American artist-designers and craftsmen who have left us a great heritage of beauty in their cut and engraved objects of art. Their distinct and original modes of expression will long be remembered and appreciated.

ACKNOWLEDGMENTS

The prolonged, intensive research of Dorothy Daniel shown in her book *Cut and Engraved Glass* pioneered the way for the exploration and appraisal of American cut glass. Prior to that publication, the absence of available reference and the idea of dealing with the thousands of patterns cut presented what seemed too formidable a task. We acknowledge our indebtedness to her for leading the way and for many years we have recommended her book to our dealers and collectors. It is now time to add new light and information to the work already accomplished.

To Leland A. Cook of Colonia, New Jersey, we express our appreciation for his superb photography. He was responsible for most of the illustrations pictured.

It is to the Historical Society of Middletown and the Wallkill Precinct, Inc., that published "Tuthill Cut Glass Co." by Mrs. Martin Rosenblum, that we owe most of the factual information on that company. The Society has performed a fine service and is justly proud in its continuing awareness of the history and contributions of that area. Mrs. Marjorie E. Purdy, secretary of the Middletown Chamber of Commerce first called our attention to the Tuthill articles published in the Middletown *Times Herald* and that newspaper very graciously has permitted us to quote and otherwise use them. Janis Tusten Horton, antique dealer, whose shop is in Middletown, N.Y., contributed valuable assistance in the research of that material. We are grateful to her for giving us further data and to Mrs. Doris Powell (daughter of Charles and Jennie Burt Tuthill), Ralph "Mike" Salvati and Harry Holmbraker (the latter two former employees of the Tuthill Co.) for giving us their personal reminiscences about Tuthill glass.

We acknowledge the assistance of and the use of material made available by the New York Historical Society (and personally the help of Nancy M. Hale of the Society), the Corning Museum of Glass and the Brooklyn Museum. Mr. Donald T. Bonnell, of the Public Relations Department of the Corning Glass Works, kindly brought to my attention the article on Sinclaire in the Corning *Leader* and that publication generously made available the information contained therein.

Among the publications we found interesting and informative were the article on the Corning Glass Works appearing in *Forbes* issue of February 1, 1962, the references to glass by the *World Book Encyclopedia*, "Christian Dorflinger, A Miracle in Glass" published by the Wayne County Historical Society, Honesdale, Pa., "C. Dorflinger & Sons" by Paul J. Fitzpatrick in the *Spinning Wheel* issue for December, 1964, *The Drama of Glass* by Kate Field, published by the Libbey Glass Co., *19th Century British Glass* by Hugh Wakefield, *Modern Glass* by Ada Polak, *Nine-*

teenth Century Glass by Albert Christian Revi, *Modern Fine Glass* by Leloise D. Skelly and *Sick Glass* by Harold J. Lagergren, translated from the Swedish by John Bottinger.

We express our thanks to Lillian Nassau, an authority on Tiffany art glass for her advice on that subject and to those collectors and dealers who made available objects owned by them for purposes of illustration.

In addition to Crockery and Glass Journals and the records of the United States Patent Office, the author has had access to the catalogues of the T. G. Hawkes Co., the Libbey Glass Co., C. Dorflinger & Sons, the Pairpoint Corp., the Fry Cut Glass Co., the Sterling Cut Glass Co., the O. F. Egginton Co. and the Mount Washington Glass Co.

The above list of acknowledgments is, of course, not complete and we express generally our appreciation to all those whose encouragement and help made this book possible.

Preface

THE United States probably has millions of discriminating collectors of glass. Comparatively few, of course, are aware that they are serious or latent collectors. Typical examples are the fastidious women who buy costly perfumes or men who buy expensive liquors. The manufacturers have knowingly contrived costly glass containers of great beauty that consciously or unconsciously influence the purchase of their products. These consumers often continue to use those containers after the contents have been exhausted or dispose of them with reluctance. Even the purchase of ordinary tableware, stemware or electrical fixtures of glass requires the use of discrimination as to color, shape or design.

In the last ten years, interest in all kinds of old glass has increased tremendously, particularly in American glass of the "Brilliant Period," about 1880 to 1915. While dealing principally with glass of that period, this book also includes for purposes of comparison references to glass made before and after.

When we were first married, my wife's possessions included some sterling candlesticks and cut glass bowls and pitchers she had inherited from her mother and grandmother. I must confess that as to the cut glass, my reaction was that it was "junk," obsolete and without merit. The cut glass was without designs I could grasp, without shapes or forms that to me could be regarded as anything but "commercial."

As our finances improved, so did our desire for the more unusual, the finer more brilliant cuts and designs more interestingly conceived. Even my son Leonard, then only seven years old, became interested when my wife decided to solve her lack-of-space problem by becoming a mail order dealer to rid herself of surplus stock. Today, at the age of 18, Leonard is one of the most knowledgeable persons on cut glass and other antiques as well. He contributed valuable aid in the research of material.

We have endeavored to read and learn first hand all we could, depending to a large extent on patent information, crockery and glass journals, catalogues, antique magazines and other records available describing the various items, designs and patterns. In addition, the practical experience of purchasing thousands of pieces as dealer and collector has, we hope, sharpened our sensitivity as to what is most desirable and collectible, though this must necessarily be a subjective judgment.

Unless otherwise noted, all of the items pictured are from the personal collection of my wife and myself. Signed pieces generally may be taken as authentic evidence of the work of the particular glass house. Included are many pieces that are so rare that few persons know that they even exist.

For the beginner, a brief sketch of background history and patterns comparatively easy to recognize are given. Also how to know, collect and care for fine cut glass. For the advanced collector and those who like to delve into the more esoteric aspects we have included the more difficult designs and variations.

In planning this book, we have tried to accomplish three objectives. First, the research of material not already contained in other publications. Unfortunately, there are too many blank spaces, information is often fragmentary and authenticity uncertain. In many instances patterns were not named, others involved variations too slight to be worth noting. Where a design was not named, we have used or invented a generic name that would describe best the general idea or the basic motif used. The use of such names is indicated by quote marks around it. This would seem to be preferable to the use of a patent number which in and of itself would do nothing to help recall the nature of the pattern. Besides, many if not most designs were not patented.

Secondly, we have tried to avoid a dry recital of factual information and data. Too many readers may understandably not be equal to the drudgery of reading them. More important is the aesthetic and artistic fabric into which these details were woven. At the same time, we have not hesitated to borrow information from others of a pertinent or explanatory nature. No writer of a technical subject can avoid doing otherwise.

Third, with only an amateur background, an attempt has been made to show directly through photography the ultimate object of our interest, its shape, design, and size, in addition to showing the patent drawing when available. Many sources have been sifted in the hope of including only that which may be regarded as truly authentic. Nevertheless one cannot rule out the possibility that the source itself may not be entirely free of error. One should therefore always keep an "open" mind for further investigation where possible.

In selecting the best of cut and engraved glass, we have tried to capture the aura of aesthetic beauty that so often inspired the craftsmen. It was created by people to be appreciated by other people and the personal element in the manufacture, use and appreciation of these fine objects of art is a very important consideration. The discriminating collector must also be aware of the fact that just as in any other art, comparatively little of it reaches those heights of originality and aesthetic force worth noting in the passing parade.

J. Michael Pearson

Brooklyn, N.Y.

CONTENTS

AMERICAN CUT GLASS

For The Discriminating Collector

Glass and Its Early History

WHAT is glass and when was it first made? The forces of nature created glass long before man learned the secret. When lightning strikes sand, the heat fuses it into long slender glass tubes called fulgurites—commonly called petrified lightning. Also, when the terrific heat of a volcanic eruption fuses rocks and sands into glass, it is called obsidian. Early man used it for knives, arrowheads, jewelry and money.

The basic ingredient of glass is that common, inexpensive raw material so plentiful everywhere—sand (silica). It usually constitutes about fifty to seventy per cent of the mix. Most of it comes from sandstone quarries where it is dug out by huge power shovels, crushed and then thoroughly washed. Then, depending on the special qualities desired, solvents are added in the form of potash, soda ash, lime, litharge, nitre, etc. Addition of decolorizing agents such as manganese and arsenic neutralize the impurities found in the sand, particularly iron particles. Lead and lime are of such importance in determining the quality of the glass that the final product is usually classified as either lead or lime glass, depending on the ingredient used. The lead product has a brilliant finish, is heavy, has a resonant ring and is the foundation of most genuine cut glass. When colored glass is desired, various metallic oxides are introduced.

The Corning Glass Works has developed more than 50,000 kinds of glass, sometimes as fine as a cobweb or as heavy as iron, as soft as cotton or as hard as diamonds. Other large glass companies such as Libbey-Owens-Ford and Owens Illinois have also done considerable research and experimentation.

When, where and how man first discovered how to make glass is a moot question and no one can be certain of the answer. Quoting from a Libbey catalogue (about 1892) we are told that: "In the metropolis of Sakkara, in ancient Memphis (Egypt) archaeologists have discovered a mortuary chapel on whose front are sculptured designs representing glass blowers at work, which were made 3,900 years before Christ or 5,700 years ago; and on the old rock tombs of Thebes you may see pictures of artisans blowing shapes of glass through long pipes. It was in these same ruins that a Captain Hervey, a British officer, picked up the round glass bead of a necklace covered with hieroglyphics, showing that fifteen hundred years before the Christian era it belonged to Queen Ramaka, the consort of Thoutmes III."

In apparent contradiction to the above quote, the *World Book Encyclopedia* (1959) says that the blowpipe was invented by some unknown artisan

15

about 300 B.C. and that as a result, the manufacture of glass became less expensive and the use of it more widespread. It is more likely that 300 B.C. marked the re-discovery of the blowpipe rather than its initial origin.

Fairly definite evidence shows that glass was made in northern Mesopotamia about 2000 B.C. Definite Egyptian records, such as the blue glass bottle of Thoutmes III in the British Museum, date back to 1550 B.C. At Tel-el-Amarna, Sir Flinders Petrie unearthed several complete glass factories which apparently operated about 1370 B.C. The Phoenicians were among the first people to produce and utilize glass commercially. They produced beads, bottles, vases and other pieces most of which were made of an opaque, non-reflecting glass.

It is known that from about 1500 B.C. until at least 300 B.C. Egypt was the centre of pressed glass made in open moulds. Rome succeeded to the art of Egypt by right of conquest. When Caesar Augustus exacted a tribute of wares and ornaments from the Egyptians, the Romans were so charmed with their beauty that they transplanted the industry to their own country. Nero, the first great collector of glassware, was a generous patron of the artists and delighted to see his banquet table glittering with their masterpieces.

Glass manufacture flourished in all the countries under Roman rule. They knew how to make relatively clear, transparent glass with offhand blowing, painting and gilding. They also knew how to build up layers of glass of different colors and then cut out designs in high relief. The celebrated Portland vase was made in Rome about 70 A.D.

After Rome, Constantinople and Venice followed in glassmaking and from Venice the art gradually spread over Europe. "The glass industry was the only one in which noblemen, to whom all labor meant degradation, could give themselves up without lowering themselves; glass workers were gentlemen." (Edmund Haraucourt in *Medieval Manners Illustrated* at the Cluny Museum). Glassmaking has practically always been considered a respected art of high social standing. For a long time, first Venetian and then later, Bohemia glass stood dominant.

It was in 1675 that George Ravenscroft, with the assistance of the Italian De Costa, produced "flint glass" by the addition of lead oxide to ordinary glass ingredients. From simple motifs like rose branches, butterflies, moths, etc., the cutting and engraving advanced by 1800 to the prismatic cuts; convex, raised diamond patterns and other intricate operations. When steam took over the task of whirling the cutting discs and grinding wheels more and deeper cutting became practicable. The result was greater brilliancy and more varied prismatic effects. It is this type of glass that became the basis for cut glass in America.

Cut and Engraved Glass in America 1812-1915

THE decoration of glass by cutting goes back to at least five or six hundred years before the birth of Christ. No attempt is made here to cover the early American periods of glassmaking or cutting about which much has been written in many other publications.

The type of cutting with which most people today are familiar did not become practical until lead oxide glass (flint) was produced. As early as 1812 the Crown Glass Co. was producing flint glass in Boston. By 1813 Bakewell and Page was doing the same in Pittsburgh, Pennsylvania. In Cramer's "Navigator" for 1813 it states that "glass-cutting is likewise executed in this place, not inferior to the best cut-glass in Europe." In 1818 the New England Glass Co. of Boston had in operation two flint glass furnaces and twenty-four cutting wheels. Early glass before 1825 lacked originality, embodying for the most part ideas and designs of foreign workers and European ideas of decoration. Much of it resembled the Irish Waterford glass made from 1729 to 1851 and the English glass of the same period. Examples of American cut glass circa 1830 are included in this book for purposes of comparison.

By 1865, glass houses near Boston were manufacturing glass equal in quality to the best flint made in England. Flint glass was also being made in other parts of the country and particularly around Pittsburgh where conditions involving raw materials and fuel favored the continuance of the type of flint glass begun by Bakewell and Page.

Between 1880 and 1890 the first large scale production of cut glass appeared. It enjoyed a widespread popularity that continued until just before World War I. The closely cut, deep and more intricate designs of the "Brilliant Period" (1880-1915) were made possible for the first time by the use of natural gas and later petroleum. This gave better control over temperatures required for more perfect fusion of the glass. The discovery of finer sand almost free of iron oxide and other technological improvements also contributed to the making of glass that was purer, more brilliant and that could be cut more precisely.

During the "Brilliant Period" business conditions were generally good. People had both the money and inclination for fine cut glass that could be shown proudly to advantage where elegance of decoration was desired at elaborate social gatherings.

American cut glass for the first time developed a new, completely original style, and designs unlike anything that had ever been produced anywhere else before. Sometimes a firm would offer cash prizes to the workman who designed a pattern that proved most popular when placed on the market.

The labor employed in cutting glass was considered highly skilled and well paid. In 1897 American glass cutters were earning as much as $18.00 a week against from $7.00 to $8.00 a week in England, $5.00 to $6.00 in France and Belgium and still less in Germany and Bohemia. But in spite of the higher cost of labor here, greater skill and more efficient methods permitted the industry to hold the home market against foreign competition.

Ralph ("Mike") Salvati, a former "smoother" for the Tuthill Glass Co. in Middletown, N.Y. (1900-1923) told us in 1961 that beginners (apprentices) started at only 5¢ an hour or $3.00 a week and that the work week was 10 hours a day, six days a week. Only the most expert cutters received the $18.00 to $20.00 a week scale.

Paul Pachuta, one of the very few experts cutting glass today, operates a shop in New York City for new glass and repairs of old. He tells us that today a glass cutter commands at least $3.00 and as much as $5.00 an hour depending on the degree of his skill.

On this basis, cut glass which was always expensive would have to sell at a retail cost of at least ten times the prices it brought when made at that time. In 1897, typical selling prices were: "Punch bowl with silver foot and border $400.00; salad bowls from $30.00 to $60.00; decanters with heavy silver stoppers at $100.00 a pair; a loving cup for $27.00; a tantalus set of three bottles with bronze bar which locks the set from tampering by servants at $60.00" etc. (from *Crockery and Glass Journal*, April, 1897.)

The history and background of some of the more important glass houses with examples of their products and designs are briefly outlined in another part of this book.

Manufacture of Glass (1880-1915)

IN the making of glass that was later to be engraved or cut, the most important item after choosing a fine grade of sand suited for the purpose was oxide of lead or red lead. The remaining materials, with variations by different companies, were potash, saltpetre and nitrate of soda. The materials were put into the mixing bins in the order in which they have been named. They were then mixed by workmen with shovels and after being turned several times and being sifted were put into the melting pots and subjected to intense heat for thirty to thirty-six hours. It required a temperature of 2,500 degrees to flux a glass mixture, while the temperature in the furnaces was generally kept at a higher degree, being about 3,000 degrees Fahrenheit.

When the glass mixture was exactly the right temperature, a "gatherer," as he was termed, ran a long, hollow pipe into the molten mass. Turning the iron over and over, he would gather on the end of the pipe the amount of glass to be blown. He would then immediately pass it to the blower.

The blowpipe consisted of a hollow iron tube, usually from four to five feet in length and varied in diameter from the thickness of a lead pencil to one and a quarter inches, according to the weight and size of the piece to be blown. Round vessels, such as goblets, tumblers, vases, etc., were blown free while square, flat pieces such as bonbon dishes, punch bowls and articles without a handle were often blown into a paste mold. In such an event, the blower mounted a wooden box, placed the molten ball into a mold having the shape of the article wanted, expanded his cheeks and began to blow. A huge bubble would appear and the glass would take on the desired form. He continued expanding it by blowing, re-heating it in the "glory hole" of a small furnace when necessary until it was in full contact with the mold.

When blowing the glass without a mold, the molten glass was lengthened by swinging or shortened by holding the pipe upright. The hollow pipe was then replaced by a solid iron rod and the workman would mold the glass with wooden tools into any shape he pleased.

The piece would then be placed into a lower heat about 900 degrees Fahrenheit, remaining there for some hours. It thus received the vital "temper" needed to lessen the chances of the piece bursting in the decorator's hands. The glass had to be cooled very gradually. The heavier pieces required as much as a week, the lighter ones about two days. The blank at this stage was known as a "plain" blank as distinguished from a "figured" blank in which a design was pressed into the glass while in a semi-fluid state.

The finest pieces of cut glass were made of good quality lead glass blanks either blown offhand or blown into a paste mold. Since the inner surface set in the air, its refractory surface was not impaired by anything touching it.

Cut glass houses were often careful to point out in their advertising that they did *not* use "figured" or "pressed" blanks. It was explained that this short cut process dulled the prismatic effect, clouded the color and subdued the sparkle of the glass. It was indeed a poor substitute for the genuine article.

Cutting and Engraving During the "Brilliant Period" (1880-1915)

THE glass blank when ready for cutting was first marked with the general lines of the pattern. Sometimes it was divided into squares with the aid of calipers. Other times some of the detail was left unmarked to allow the cutter some freedom in the execution of the design.

In deep cutting, the first workman to handle the blank after the pattern had been traced was the "rougher." He used steel wheels of varying sizes called "mills" which had a sharp, mitred edge. It gave the first important cuts of the design. Above the wheel of every cutter was a funnel from which wet sand dripped constantly upon the wheel. The combination of sand and whirling wheel ground the glass down to the proper depth. It took long practice to acquire the necessary skill. Five years had to be spent in an apprenticeship.

The glass was then given to the "smoother" who used special stones imported from Scotland and England. They were known by the old county names of Yorkshire Flag, New Castle and Craigleith. They were very hard, close grained and capable of retaining a very sharp edge. With these, the worker made the very fine cuts, stars, crosses, fans, small diamonds, scallops, etc. He also refined the lines made by the rougher restoring their translucency. The stone was mitred to the same angle as the cuts so that he could hold the blank upon the face of the wheel. An intricate design often required many days of constant manipulation. To prevent shattering of the glass, a lump of wet clay was sometimes held inside the object to absorb the vibration of the wheels. Dripping water from an overhead suspended hopper kept the emery wheels wet and cool.

To obtain the best results, polishing was done in three stages. First, it was done with wooden wheels fed with pumice, stone and water; then brush or wool wheels with the same preparation, and lastly cork or felt wheels with finely compounded putty powder. About the turn of the century, the acid bath, quicker and less expensive came into use for polishing. It was hand-burnishing, however, that gave the superb brilliance down to the smallest detail.

Engraving is cutting requiring copper wheels, some of them as dainty as a diamond. Linseed oil and pumice are used instead of the coarser abrasives. This method made possible a different type of minutely detailed decoration,

21

usually left unpolished with a gray white surface. When polished some companies called it "Rock Crystal" being imitative of the natural quartz of that name.

The decorator of an engraved piece might either outline his design upon the glass or might start directly with the wheel, developing it with independence as an artist might in painting. Engraving generally was used for realistic subjects rather than for the geometric patterns.

Intaglio glass is cut glass which is "carved" out deeply or "sculptured," usually but not always left unpolished. This type of cutting gives depth and perspective to the subject matter and the silver gray finish is in sharp contrast to the rest of the piece which is polished. The H. P. Sinclaire Co., Libbey, Hawkes and Tuthill, to name a few, did exceptional work in intaglio which many consider the highest form of the cutter's art. The Hawkes company, for a brief period after 1900 did intaglio of exceptional merit called "Hawkes Gravic Glass." The iris, carnation and astor flowers and mitre and fruit were the usual subjects. Many examples of intaglio glass by these companies are illustrated in this book. Every collection of fine cut glass should include at least one or two pieces although they are not plentiful and may be expensive. When acquiring this type of glass, the amount of detail and nuances in the shading, originality of style and precision of the cutting should be major considerations in addition to the quality and form of the glass used.

The Aesthetic Appreciation of
Cut Glass As an Art

NO other substance created by nature or man is capable of a greater variety of expression than glass. Men have used it to express feelings of beauty ever since they first learned how to make it. In prismatic form it can pick the component colors of the spectrum out of ordinary light; it can rival the natural diamond in color and brilliance so that a jeweler will need his eye piece to distinguish it. The play of light on fine clear glass properly displayed has nuances of infinite variety. The words "crystal clear" or "pure as crystal" express as no other words can the feelings that glass inspire. When color, form and decoration, either cut or applied are used, the possibilities are endless.

While most people regard craftsmanship as applied to cut glass as an industrial art, there are many examples of cut, engraved, intaglio and cameo glass that go far beyond this designation and constitute art in the true sense of the word—the application of skill and taste to express aesthetic principles. This is especially so of the engraved and intaglio work of such glass houses as Hawkes, Libbey, Sinclaire and Tuthill. The use of intaglio engraving particularly permits depth and perspective for realistic and literary subject matter.

To some, the geometric patterns are too intricate and difficult to grasp as an entirety. In this day and age of abstract and surrealistic art, most of the public is already sufficiently bewildered to cry "uncle" and retreat to the nearest psychiatrist's couch. In their distress, they plead for the clear and simple reality that is certainly not less worthy because it is easily understood. Beauty, like truth, can be simple as well as abstruse.

It is important however, to bear in mind that the legitimate scope of art ranges from the subtle and complex to the simple and obvious. There is room for honest, genuine appreciation in all its aspects. Those who set limitations on artistic expression are more likely to expose their own limitations.

Primarily, the purpose of many of the geometric designs of the "Brilliant Period" was to show the purity and brilliance of the glass. Minor line variations of many of the patterns that are similar are more likely to be of purely esoteric interest to those who like to probe as to its origin. But many designs, such as "Chrysanthemum," "Bullseye," "Comet," "Drape," "Pinetree," "Stalks and Stars" and the "Shell" patterns, to name a few, are definite conceptions to which the sensitive viewer can readily respond. Oscar

23

Wilde once said, "The facts of art are diverse but the essence of artistic effect is *unity.*" Other geometric patterns go much further into the abstract. For those who enjoy thinking in such terms, the geometric patterns may have the greater appeal. On the other hand, those who dislike abstractions and are confused by anything not realistic and objective, will prefer the engraved and intaglio work showing animals, flowers, birds, insects, etc., and conventionalized versions of these categories. It will also be a question of to what degree and how far in each direction a person's feelings run. It is purely a matter of personal taste and great art work has been accomplished in both areas.

How to Collect American Cut Glass

ONE of the questions most commonly asked is what should a person collect and how should one judge quality.

The beginner would do best picking a particular category, e.g., tumblers, cruets, knife rests or miniatures or by concentrating on one or two designs that are considered desirable. Generally, the finest glass has a heavy lead oxide content whether you pick early American flint, "Middle Period" or "Brilliant Period." The earlier glass will usually have minor imperfections, tiny bubbles, striae, or many even show very fine grains of sand. Of course this is not necessarily always so. This was due to impurities in the metal and less perfect fusion as well as the inability of the maker to control the exact temperatures required for fusion until natural gas came into use as fuel. It will, however, ring with a bell-like tone unless the piece has a closed top as do decanters, bottles and other heavy narrow tops or in other cases where the nature of the piece smothers the ring. It should readily respond to a tap with a pencil or a snap of the finger when held lightly at the bottom center. You can even get a good sound out of the thicker part, for example the handles, of the finer early flint glass.

Lead glass is usually heavy and thick, permitting sharper, deeper incisions and greater variety of designs. It is the "Brilliant Period" glass that has the exceptional silver whiteness and Steuben-like purity and luminous color. The designs of the "Brilliant Period" were original and distinctive, unlike any glass ever cut before or since except for some present day imitations of comparatively poor quality being cut in West Germany which are lighter in weight, shallow cut with the fine line cutting usually left an unpolished gray. The glass itself has a lifeless color with a superficial shiny surface lustre.

Fine cut glass is sharp to the touch with perfection of line and design. Cheaper, poorly executed cuts will show in irregular spaced lines and imbalance in the design. Glass polished on wooden wheels has a more lustrous appearance with less imperfections on the surface. Rottenstone and pumice also give a satin-like finish. After 1900 acid polishing was often used resulting in a finish that was not as expensive and quicker. To most collectors however, the hand polishing is more desirable and the softer, smoother luster without the lacquer-like finish of acid polishing more attractive.

Glass cut on pressed blanks should be avoided. You can readily determine whether such a blank has been used by feeling the inside part opposite the deeper incisions. Raised ridges will be felt where the glass was pressed by the plunger while in a semifluid state, causing a loss of refractive qualities in the blank and in the final result after cutting.

You should decide on whether you want rare cabinet pieces and designs or larger pieces and those cut in such large quantities that you may more readily collect "sets." Or you may prefer to collect colored American cut glass, a more difficult pursuit that should be undertaken by only the more advanced and affluent collector since it is likely to be expensive and it is not always easy to be sure of its origin. A beginner may be better off buying from a knowledgeable, reliable dealer who will guarantee authenticity.

The essential tool for learning patterns is the motif chart. The ability to pick the one or two dominant motifs will often enable you to remember the fundamental character of the design. Usually a nappy or bowl in your possession will fix the pattern in your mind better than any drawing, diagram or picture.

If there are serious chips in the pattern itself, it is usually much less desirable. Chips on rim surfaces and in the clear portions are less serious and more easily smoothed down and corrected. Whenever you buy pieces having handles, be sure to check the handles where they are joined to the main body. Too often the annealing (cooling) process or a struck handle will result in inside cracks not obvious on a hasty, superficial inspection. If buying a butter or cheese dish or a punch bowl or any other item of two or more pieces, make sure that they are not mismatched. The basic motifs should be identical in all the pieces of the ensemble.

Do not buy bottles or decanters or other narrow neck pieces that are greyed or discolored unless you are sure that the piece will be clear after cleansing and drying. While it is best to buy "mint" (perfect) pieces, a truly rare item should be bought where the price is adequately discounted in proportion to the seriousness of the defect.

Many persons like to buy signed pieces as a guaranty of authenticity. This does not necessarily follow as we have seen the Hawkes acid etched trademark on inferior glass that were either very "late" or forgeries. The Hawkes catalogues always made much of the fact that "pressed" blanks were *never* used by that company. Their advertising also boasted the same and until recently, we had never seen the Hawkes mark on a pressed blank. The design and quality of the cutting were also so poor as to raise some doubts of their being the genuine article. Once you have determined from an authentic piece, signed, that it was cut by a certain company, you may assume that the identical pattern though unsigned, was cut by the same company. Though patents were often copied and infringed upon, the company doing the copying rarely failed to make some slight variation as a defense against a possible lawsuit.

26

To summarize, buy the piece having elegant form or unique shape, with purity and brilliance of color, sharpness of edges and precision of cutting, heavy bell-tone response to touch, deep cut with the aesthetic appeal of a well organized integrated pattern. The early patterns of the "Brilliant Period" were usually deep, over-all cut and, because of that, more brilliant. On the other hand, some of the later cuts were not only brilliant in spite of less surface being cut, but the designs were more interesting, less intricate and with greater aesthetic appeal. Some of the finest intaglio cut glass ever made belongs to this later period. If your prospective purchase meets all the tests we have outlined above, buy it even if you have never seen the pattern or anything like it anywhere else before.

The Care and Display of Fine Cut Glass

THERE is as much difference in the color of glass, meaning only transparent colorless glass or crystal, as there is in the color of diamonds, and the beauty and value of the glass as well as the stone are measured very largely by its perfection in this respect.

Fine glass should be of a purity that practically renders it invisible without any trace of yellow or green cast or opacity. Sometimes it will have a slightly bluish white color. Glassware that defies casual criticism as regards color when seen by itself will often appear to a decided disadvantage when placed beside a really fine piece.

Cut glass should be washed one piece at a time in tepid water using a castile soap and working the lather into the cutting with a soft brush, a toothbrush serving very well for the purpose. It should then be dried without draining on a soft towel. When perfectly dry, the cut surfaces should be gone over with a clean dry brush that will penetrate every crevice of the pattern. A soft, lint-free cloth should then be used to give it a high polish.

For cleansing the inside of water bottles or other narrow necked vessels, add rice (uncooked) to a solution of muriatic (hydrochloric) acid or to vinegar and shake it vigorously. Oiliness may be removed with alcohol left in for about 15 minutes after which it should be dried and rinsed with water. In some cases, using a tea bag with vinegar will give good results if left to soak overnight.

One authority suggests that discoloration caused by perfume, wine or other liquids in decanters, cruets, etc., may be removed by allowing chopped potato peel with a small amount of water to stand in a bottle overnight, then emptying and washing with water.

Glass which continues to cloud up after cleaning and rinsing is known as "sick glass." It is caused by the formation and separation of crystals due to imperfect fusion of the metal or too high an alkaline content in the making. It can be professionally polished off and then "glass wax" applied if the area can be reached. Frequent applications of the wax will be helpful in delaying further deterioration. Unfortunately, this remedy is usually not practical where it is needed most—in the cleansing of bottle type containers.

The use of ammonia or strongly alkaline soaps should be avoided. Extreme and sudden changes of temperature may also be harmful. Before using ice-cream platters, punch bowls, sherbet glasses or other pieces designed for frozen foods or chilled beverages, the glass should be allowed to stand for a few minutes in a cold place or held under a jet of cold water.

Cut glass with sterling silver mountings was once very popular. To this very day, many people consider the use of sterling articles with cut glass as the basis for the most elegant table settings.

TERMINOLOGY

Bars of cane—see plate 20

Beading

Chain of hobstars

Blaze

Block

Chain of hobstars alternating with cross cut diamond

Bullseye (also called punty)
see plates 39, 40, 41, 42

Checkered diamond

Button—hobnail hexagon or octagon figure, with or without decoration

Cluster

Buzz (see pinwheel),
also see plate 51

Cameo—cut so as to produce design in relief

Copper wheel engraving—glass cut by use of small copper wheels and usually polished to a high "rock crystal" finish

Cane— (same as chairbottom)
see plate 30

Cross – cut   diamond

Cross hatched—cut in parallel or cross lines.

Cased—refers to glass in which one or more layers are enclosed in outside layer which is usually of a different color

Center radiants

Diamond shaped field—

Fan

Feather

Fern

Flashed—coating of colored glass with design cut through to clear or to another color

Flashed fan

Flashed hobstar

Flute—similar to panel but sometimes vertical is concave (hollowed out), examples—
see tankard pitcher, plate 162

Fringe (see Blaze)

Hexagon—six sided figure also called hobnail or "button"

Hobnail—raised hexagon or octagon figure, also called "button"

Hobnail chain—hobnail figures joined to encircle figure or design

Hobstar

Hobstar chain—hobstar figures joined to encircle figure or design, see "Chain of hobstars"

Hobstar in diamond field—hobstar enclosed in 4 sided figure in shape of diamond

Horizontal step cutting

Lozenge shaped, 6 sided, 5 sided

Nailhead diamond—relief diamond with four sides

Panel—similar to flute but usually refers to flat vertical rather than the concave hollowed out verticals

Pillar—raised and rounded out **convex** prism

Pinwheel (same as buzz)
see plate 51

Prism—a cut bar, mitred on long edges, see plates 37, 38, 39 and 40

Punty (same as bullseye)

Pyramidal star

Radiant—design lines or figures extending from a set point

Relief diamond—four sided diamond cut so as to appear raised from surface of the glass

Rock crystal—natural quartz mineral, but term is used as a trade name for glass imitation of it

Rosettes—used to describe hobstar or modified versions of it.

Saint Louis Diamond—large concave diamond shaped figure, also called "honeycomb"
see Dorflinger pitcher, plate 103

Scalloped—border consisting of a series of circle segments usually radially

ribbed with fan and having an undulated (serrated) edge, see plate 15

Serrated edge—sawtooth or dentil edge—see edge of tray, plate 15

Single star

Star center

Split—acute angle cut

Split vesica
see plate 62

Step cutting (see horizontal step cutting)

Strawberry diamond

Teardrop—bubble of air deliberately placed inside the glass as an embellishment

Vesica—a pointed oval
see plate 62

"X" split vesica
see plate 32

LIST OF PATTERN ILLUSTRATIONS BY PLATE NUMBER

Cut Glass

PATTERNS

RUSSIAN PATTERN

Courtesy of the Corning Museum of Glass

Plate 13¾ inches in diameter, cut by T. G. Hawkes & Co., Corning, New York. Exhibited at Columbian Exposition, Chicago, Illinois.

PLATE 1

1. RUSSIAN PATTERN

This pattern was designed by Philip MacDonald, a cutter for Thomas G. Hawkes. It was patented June 20, 1882, patent number 12982 and assigned to his employer.

This design was chosen for a complete banquet service to be cut for the Russian Embassy in Washington, D.C., and has been known as the "Russian" pattern ever since. It won wide and popular acceptance.

A second complete service was ordered in the same design in 1885 for use at the American Embassy in St. Petersburg and in 1886 the White House in Washington adopted the pattern with the engraved eagle crest added to it. The service was maintained with additions as required and appeared as late as 1938 during the administration of Franklin D. Roosevelt. Because it was too expensive, it was later discontinued and replaced by a less costly service.

As explained in the patent papers: "It is obvious that any figure may be cut on the hexagonal or 'hob-nail.' ". . . on these broad faces a figure is cut to suit the taste of the artist." Thus, the hobnail or "button" part of the design was varied: 1. sometimes clear (undecorated), 2. cut with single star (Canterbury), 3. cut in strawberry diamond (Ambassador) and 4. cut with a many pointed hobstar (Persian).

Pieces cut on high quality lead blanks in this pattern were usually deep and full cut giving an exceptionally brilliant result. Because so much glass was cut in this pattern, persons desiring to collect sets should do well with it. Practically all the other glass houses later cut variations which often included other motifs as well.

A. Low bowl, 9" diameter. Button is starred.
B. Large cookie jar, height 9", including cut knob on cover; button is starred.

PLATE 2

RUSSIAN PATTERN

Pair of Russian cut candelabra (star button), standard has knobbed teardrop and swirl design, very rare and probably made only on special order.

PLATE 3

RUSSIAN PATTERN

Covered butter dish—clear button. Decanter, over-all height including stopper 10¾", cut with clear button with flute cutting near lip.

Oval tray, approx. 13¾" x 10", button has clear center with hobstar around it.

Covered butter tub with fitted cover and matching plate (star button).

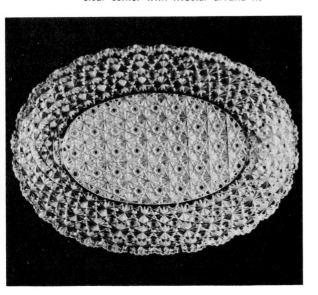

PLATE 4

RUSSIAN PATTERN

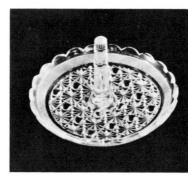

TOP ROW: A. Kidney shaped bowl, clear button (Pairpoint); B. Stick dish with crosshatched band; C. Perfume bottle.

LOWER ROW: D. Two piece cake stand (very rare), strawberry diamond button, teardrop stem, has 32 point hobstar base; E. Leaf dish; F. Milk pitcher, 8″ tall with unusual raised lip, squared handle cut in hobnail.

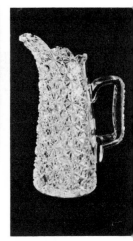

Plate 5

2. PARISIAN

Patented on May 4, 1886 #16676, by John S. O'Connor for C. Dorflinger & Sons by whom he was employed as designer and cutting shop foreman.

This simple but effective design consists of curved splits with strawberry diamond and fan alternating opposite fans above the splits. Note the beaded line separating the motifs. This was one of the first patterns to use the curved miter split. Frequent use of it characterized Dorflinger cuttings.

Wines in this pattern, very rare, were cut in green, blue, chartreuse and topaz. Any piece in clear or color is rare and a collector's item. See jacket for example from authors' collection.

Reproduced from U.S. Patent Office files.

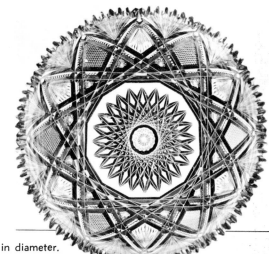

Bowl—10″ in diameter.

1. Square cordial; 2. Cordial with collar of cross-cut diamond; 3. Perfume, 6″ in height including stopper (all in Parisian pattern).

PLATE 6

3. STRAWBERRY DIAMOND & STAR

Patented June 1, 1886 #16,720 by Walter A. Wood of Honesdale, Pa. Assigned to and cut by T. B. Clark & Co. Patent drawing below of a fruit dish is reproduced from the patent office records. It consists of squares of strawberry diamond and star with a larger square formed by pyramidal diamonds in relief. ". . . At the border or periphery of the dish is disposed a series of fan-shaped scalloped figures, . . ."

Pieces in this early pattern are usually deeply and fully cut, excellent quality and wood polished to a fine patina on its brilliant surface. This is one of the choicest and most desirable patterns, highly collectible. Later, it was cut by other houses with variations including other motifs.

Reproduced from U.S. Patent Office files.

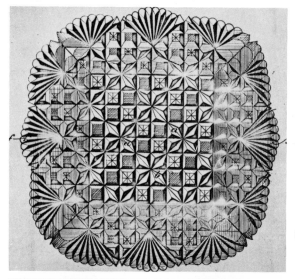

Milk pitcher, bulbous type, 5½" tall.

Plate 7½" diam, in variation, with 32-point hobstar center.

Two handled ice bucket, 6" deep.

PLATE 7

STRAWBERRY DIAMOND & STAR

Pitcher; height 8″; Carafe, square with relief diamond motif reduced in size.

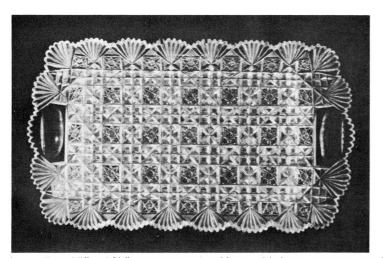 

Tray 17″ x 9½″, variation with addition of hobstar in square motif, a bowl in this design is in the exhibit of the Corning Museum of Glass; Bowling pin decanter with matching shape stopper, 15″ tall, large hobstar added.

PLATE 8

4. MIDDLESEX

Patented by William C. Anderson for the New England Glass Co., January 25, 1887 #17072. This was one of the first patterns to use the eight point hobstar as a basic motif. Illustrated below: 1. The original design of the New England Glass Co. (the barrel-shaped pitcher); 2 & 3, A cookie jar and pitcher in the Dorflinger variation; 4. The Hawkes' "Middlesex"—a handled decanter.

The New England version (very rare) has a star in the center of and around the hobstar which is framed by beading around it. The Dorflinger substitutes a four-sided strawberry diamond figure opposite the fans, the hobstar is surrounded by a field of strawberry diamond and there is no beading. The Hawkes variation has a clear hobstar center and field around it and is framed by a simple prism cutting. More of the Dorflinger was cut than the others. Practically anything in these patterns is desirable but hard to acquire.

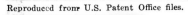
Reproduced from U.S. Patent Office files.

PLATE 9

5. GRECIAN

Designed by Thomas G. Hawkes, patented October 25, 1887 #17837. This is one of the most beautiful patterns ever cut and one of the rarest. Although it uses the pyramidal star and starred hobnail of the Russian pattern, the placement of the clear tear-shaped vesicas and the addition of the radiants between them create a brilliant contrast between the purity of the finest clear glass and the starred motifs.

A full dinner service was cut for display at the Paris Exposition in 1889 where it won the International Grand Prize. Pieces in this pattern are unsigned as the Hawkes trademark was not used until after 1890 (registered in the Copyright Office, March 3, 1903).

Perfume or cordial bottle with original diamond cut stopper.

Reproduced from Patent Office files.

Goblet in Grecian pattern, hobstar base and knobbed teardrop stem.

PLATE 10

5 A. RUSSIAN AND PILLAR

Patented October 25, 1887 (same date as the Grecian) by Thomas G. Hawkes and given patent number 17838. In his patent papers it is described as consisting of: "A series of rosettes (the pyramidal star) . . . series of small rosettes (the star button) . . . (and) the ribs or pillars on each side of the rosette portions and a bead between the ribs or pillars."

It is an effective and lovely pattern using the basic Russian motif with the addition of the swirled pillar and notched parallel lines. The quality of the glass and the cutting is the finest. Variations were cut by Hawkes himself and by other glass houses. Anything in this pattern or the better variations is a rare collector's find.

Reproduced from U.S. Patent Office files.

Decanter in variation with hobstar rosettes and tearshaped clear vesicas protruding from the rest of the glass. Note the heavy double collar and graceful shape of the large handle.

Decanter with heavy Gorham sterling top in shape of eagle's head. Flute cutting and band of hobstars added to patent design. Over-all height 14 inches. Most likely made for a special order.

Carafe in original patent design.

PLATE 11

6. HOBNAIL

The simple six-sided (hexagonal) or eight-sided (octagonal) figure referred to as "button" in the pressed glass pattern "Button and Daisy" became known as "hobnail" because it resembled the heads of nails used on old boots.

On April 24, 1888, Thomas G. Hawkes patented design #18267 which used the hobnail motif together with clear ovals and fan radiants. A comparison of the perfume bottle below, in this pattern, with the one illustrated under Grecian, Plate 10, shows that, from a side view, the patterns are similar except for the substitution of hobnail (undecorated) for the Russian motif of pyramidal star and starred button used in the Grecian. Hawkes' patent was, of course, one of the choicest and superior to the simple hobnail used without other embellishments. The latter was comparatively less expensive to produce and popular. It was cut on fine glass and, though more plentiful than most other designs, has appeal to the more conservative taste.

Patent #18267—Perfume bottle 7¾" tall including stopper.

Pitcher, 5¼" tall cut in simple hobnail.

PLATE 12

7. DEVONSHIRE

Patented May 8, 1888, by Thomas G. Hawkes, #18301. Generally, most items using the star and strawberry diamond motifs in alternate squares or diamond fields may be considered as Devonshire or a variation of it. Cuttings in this pattern were usually full cut and the over-all effect is a pleasing one.

Milk pitcher, height—6 inches.

Vase, 9 inches tall.

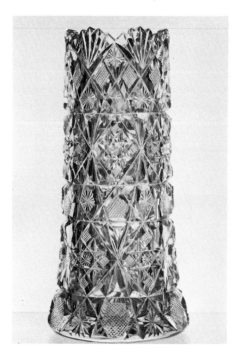

PLATE 13

8. CROSS-CUT DIAMOND & FAN

This simple pattern was cut in large quantities by most of the cutting shops. Unlike pattern 3 (Strawberry Diamond & Star) the diamond has a cross cut at the top of it instead of the closely cut strawberry diamond motif that is similar to the berry it imitates. It is better to call it Cross-cut Diamond & Fan since this name gives the actual motifs used, avoids confusion and differentiates the two patterns. Dealers often refer to this pattern as "Pineapple & Fan" because it reminds them of the surface texture of the pineapple· fruit.

The design was popular and many people chose it for its simplicity and because it was one of the least expensive. Quality varies widely and while it is easy to collect sets in this pattern, care must be taken to select only pieces that meet the tests of fine cut glass.

Tray, 7 x 10 inches and (right) Goblet in cross-cut diamond & fan.

PLATE 14

Decanter with notched handle.

Round tray, 24 point hobstar center.

"Pineapple" shaped vase, 8⅝" tall in
"Pineapple and Fan."

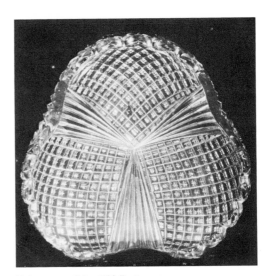

Tri-corner dish, 7½" diameter.

Plate 15

9. FLORENCE

This design was patented April 23, 1889, by William C. Anderson for Edward D. Libbey, and given patent #19053. The geometric motifs are intricately woven into a complicated pattern not easily remembered except for the large hobstar flashed with fans between the points. As a result, any pattern having the flashed hobstar in strawberry diamond is usually referred to as "Florence" although not identical to the patent and though it incorporates, to a minor extent, other motifs. In our own experience, we have seen little of the actual standard, the variations being much more common.

No. 19,053.   Patented Apr. 23, 1889.

Reproduced from U.S. Patent Office files.

Ice bucket—view looking into it to show strawberry diamond hobstar with fans between the points.

Ice bucket, Pat. 19053, 6½" diameter.

Variation, Cake stand on 3 legs 9¾" diameter.

PLATE 16

10. LOUIS XIV

Richard Briggs, of Boston, Mass., was prominent as one of the most important importers of china and glass. With practically everyone else cutting glass in the geometric patterns, he wanted to give his clientele, which included some of the wealthiest men in the country, something different. Designs patent numbers 19105 and 19106 were the result.

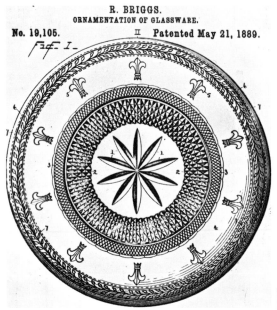

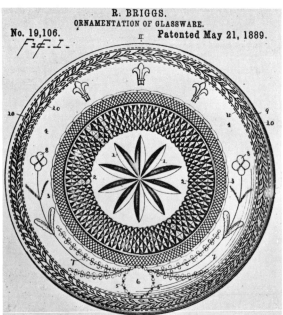

Reproduced from U.S. Patent Office files.

These simple, balanced designs containing the fleur de lis (a French Baccarat influence), were cut on fine lead glass and often included family crests, coats of arms and monograms. Sets were ordered for exclusive clubs and for owners of luxurious yachts. They were cut only by T. G. Hawkes on special orders for Richard Briggs customers.

Cuttings in this pattern are often overlooked and not recognized because the glass used is not as heavy or thick and the design not so typical of the "Brilliant Period." By being on the constant alert and diligent, a collector may be lucky enough to acquire a piece where he would least expect to find it.

Carafe, pat. 19105, 6¼" tall, Note monogram between **fleur de lis.**

Berry bowl, pat. 19106, 4¾" diam.

PLATE 17

11. STRATFORD

Stratford was patented December 3, 1889 #19450. It was designed by William C. Anderson for the Libbey Glass Co. at Toledo, Ohio. It illustrates the development of the "group motif," in this instance, the grouping of six hobstars around a hexagon split into six parts that are finely crosshatched (strawberry diamond). This group motif re-occurs frequently, was used by the H. C. Fry Glass Co. (see bowl below, lower left), and was used to build up the pattern "Arabian" by O. F. Egginton & Co. (below, lower right). Many other companies cut this type of design with variations and with other motifs added.

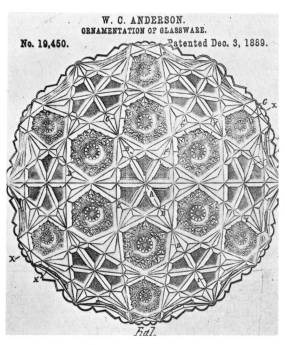

Reproduced from U.S. Patent Office files.

Tray 13½ x 8¾". Note that fan motif has been added. Handles are raised and prism cut.

Bowl signed "Fry", 9½" diameter, with 32-point hobstar center.

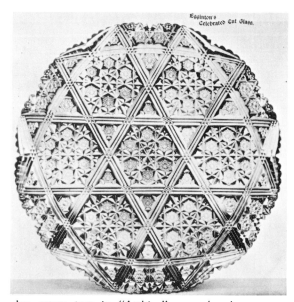

Ice cream tray in "Arabian", reproduced from O. F. Egginton catalogue.

PLATE 18

12. CLUSTER

The pattern of this name by the O. F. Egginton Co. uses the group motif of six hobstars around a six point strawberry diamond hobstar. The center is either a hobstar, as in the Egginton illustration below, or a modified hobstar (with a star center) shown in the tray. In these examples, a secondary group motif, the cross or "X" split vesica also appears. The four parts of this split vesica are usually cut in cross-cut diamond, cane, hobnail or strawberry diamond. This basic motif re-occurs in many patterns and was cut by most of the glass houses.

Tray, 8″ x 14½″.

Cluster, 8″ Low Bowl. Reproduced from catalogue of O. F. Egginton Co.

PLATE 19

13. STAR—BARS OF CANE

In this pattern, bars of cane split an enlarged hexagon central figure into six strawberry diamond segments, as in the Stratford design. These bars extend to the very tip of the larger star. Offsetting it are the huge hobstar rosettes in a clear field instead of the restricted lines of the hexagon. Variations substituted bars of hobnail or strawberry diamond instead of cane.

Ice cream tray, 10″ x 17″. Note similarity to Kimberly tray (Plate 24).

PLATE 20

14. VENETIAN

This pattern, patented June 3, 1890 by Thomas G. Hawkes is one of the most beautiful and rarest of the Brilliant Period. The use of the cross-hatched tear shaped radiants with the fan motif create a conception of expanding brilliance. The border of scalloped fans and chain of 8-point hobstars act as a frame for the large central figure. Any collector would be fortunate to acquire even a single piece.

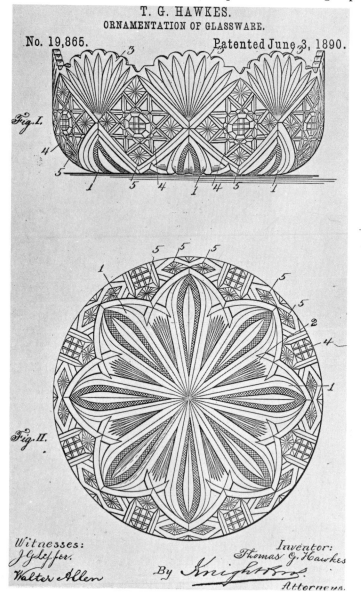

Tray, 11½" square. One similar to this is in the Smithsonian Institution.

Rose bowl 6" high, 5½" in diameter.

PLATE 21

15. CHRYSANTHEMUM

This is one of the few patterns named by the designer himself. In describing it, Hawkes wrote: "The leading features of my design consist of the large central figure having radial leaves and the flowers between the outer portions of the leaves, thus forming what I call the 'Chrysanthemum' design."

In 1889, this design was one of the entries at the Paris Exposition to win the grand international prize for cut glass. It is one of the rarest and most desirable patterns of the Brilliant Period. It was and still is, one of the most expensive to acquire, and eagerly sought after by collectors.

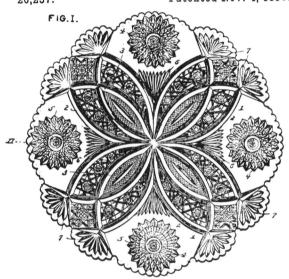

T. G. HAWKES.
ORNAMENTATION OF GLASSWARE.

20,257.   Patented Nov. 4, 1890.

FIG.I.

Reproduced from U.S. Patent Office files.

Ice cream tray, pat. #20257, 15" by 11".

Water pitcher 7" tall.

Goblet 6" tall in variation.

PLATE 22

16. WEDGEMERE

Wedgemere was patented July 7, 1891 patent #20291 by William C. Anderson for the Libbey Glass Co. At first glance it appears complicated by too many motifs. The exquisite quality of the glass and close, precise cutting make it one of the most brilliant patterns ever made.

The basic innovation is the use of large ovals that intersect and overlap each other. This is more obvious in the reproduction of the patent office design below than in the tray illustrated, which because of its shape does not lend itself so readily to the concept. In the tray, the apex of the oval (called "obovoid" by the description in the patent papers) is the tips of the radiants with the strawberry diamond checkering rather than the point of the hobstar as in the standard. The magnificent glass and skillful execution of the design make this pattern one of the very best ever cut. It is expensive and rare but worthy of a collector's diligent search.

Patent #20921—Ice cream tray, 17½" x 10½", signed "Libbey".

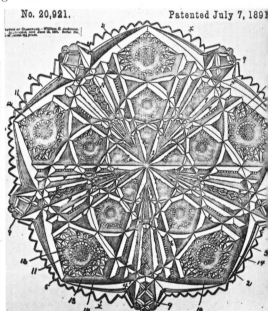

No. 20,921.   Patented July 7, 1891

Reproduced from U.S. Patent Office files.

PLATE 23

17. KIMBERLY

Design patented March 8, 1892 #21364 by William C. Anderson for the Libbey Glass Co.

The Kimberly pattern by Libbey (1890) in the Toledo Museum of Art shown in the August 1961 issue of *Woman's Day* shows a large 8-point star instead of the 6-point star illustrated here by a tray and by the reproduction of the patent office copy. Their example has a 24-point hobstar center instead of the hexagon center split into six sections. We regard the pattern here given as the standard. It is attractive—a very choice and desirable collector's item. Supply, however, seems very limited.

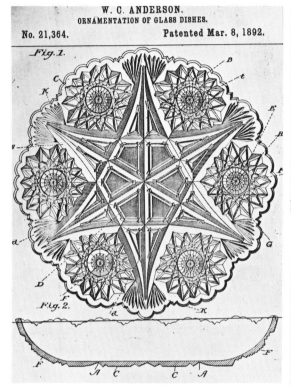

W. C. ANDERSON.
ORNAMENTATION OF GLASS DISHES.
No. 21,364.   Patented Mar. 8, 1892.
Fig.1.
Fig.2.
Reproduced from U.S. Patent Office files.

Tray, 18" x 10½", patent #21364. Part of an ice cream set that includes 6" plates.

Celery tray, 10¾" x 5" in variation with hobstar center and large extended hobstar. Outer decoration is like the standard. Note parallel line cutting in points of center hobstar.

PLATE 24

18. "RIBBON STAR" BY LIBBEY GLASS CO.

This pattern, illustrated below in the four part dish and cakestand, neither of which is signed, is identified in the *Encyclopaedia Britannica* Plate XVIa as made by the Libbey Glass Co. at Toledo, Ohio, during the period 1890-1893. The distinguishing feature is the eight-point star made up of a "ribbon" of the cane motif. Because of this, we call it "Ribbon Star." It is similar to the "Kimberly" pattern shown in *Woman's Day* on page 32 of the August, 1961, issue except that no cane is used and no hobstar is cut at the tips of the large figure in the example given in that publication.

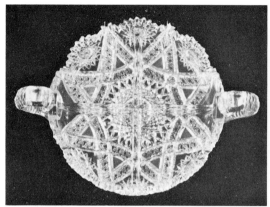

Four compartment dish, 8″ exclusive of handles.

Cake stand on a low standard, 13″ in diameter.

PLATE 25

"RIBBON STAR" VARIATION

Note that the variation illustrated below has single-star center, the hobstars are enclosed in a diamond field and the fan motif is added.

Plate, 6½″ in diameter, six-point star.

Fingerbowl, 5″ diameter, five-point star.

PLATE 26

19. WHEELER

20. HORTENSIA

21. WESTMINSTER

The Wheeler, Hortensia and Westminster patterns of the Mount Washington Glass Co., New Bedford, Massachusetts, were deeply cut sharply and precisely on thick, heavy glass of excellent quality. The items are fully cut with designs of seemingly simple but unified concepts. All of the photographs below are reproduced from an 1895 catalogue of the company except the 8½" bowl, which is part of the author's collection.

Ice Cream Tray, Wheeler

Wheeler, bowl, 8½" diam.

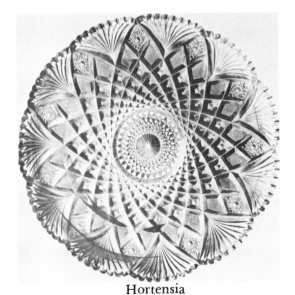

Hortensia

Skillful use of curved splits to create effect of expanding design. See also "Expanding Star" plate 61.

Ice Cream Tray, Westminster

Use of chain of alternating hobstar and cross-cut diamond with scalloped fan border.

PLATE 27

22. COLUMBIA

"Columbia" was designed by William C. Anderson for the Libbey Glass Co. patented February 14, 1893 #22213. It was exhibited at the World's Fair Columbian Exposition in Chicago in 1893, at the Libbey pavilion. It is one of the loveliest and best conceived patterns, using pillar cutting (requiring exceptional skill) to create "tusks" as one of the motifs. So little of it is available that the acquisition of a single piece is a difficult attainment.

Low bowl, 10" diameter, signed "Libbey", one hobstar edge turns inward.

22,213. ORNAMENTATION OF GLASSWARE. WILLIAM C. ANDERSON, Toledo, Ohio, assignor to the Libby Glass Company, same place. Filed Nov 19, 1892. Serial No 452,589. Term of patent 3½ years.

Claim.—The design for the ornamentation of glassware herein described and shown, the same consisting of the central stellated figure having substantially elliptical rays, each terminating in a single acute angle or point at its outer end, and the series of smaller stellated figures outside of said central figure, as set forth.

Reproduced from U.S. Patent Office files.

PLATE 28

23. BERGEN'S WHITE ROSE

"Bergen's White Rose" was designed by James D. Bergen for the J. D. Bergen Co. of Meriden, Conn., and patented May 29, 1894 #23317. Very few pieces were cut in this beautiful but comparatively simple, easily recognizable pattern. Anything in this design is a collector's item.

Reproduced from U.S. Patent Office files.

Low bowl, 8" diameter.

PLATE 29

24. CANE (ALSO KNOWN AS CHAIRBOTTOM)

Cut by most glass houses both with and without other motifs.

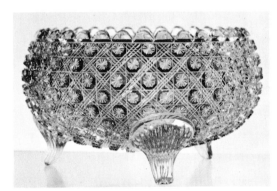

Fern bowl on legs, 9" in diameter in cane with triple mitre cutting between starred hobnail buttons. This pattern cut in quantity by Pairpoint.

Handled decanter on a standard in cane motif, 13½" tall including stopper.

PLATE 30

25. "SPLIT SQUARE"
Patented Feb. 19, 1895.

24,060. GLASS DISH. ARTHUR E. O'CONNOR, Hawley, Pa., assignor
to John S. O'Connor, same place. Filed Jan. 16, 1895. Serial No. 535,153.
Term of patent 7 years.

Reproduced from U.S. Patent Office files.

Pat. 24060, candlesticks 16" tall, 32-point
hobstar base.

PLATE 31

26. "X" SPLIT VESICA

Patented Apr. 16, 1895.

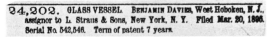

24,202. GLASS VESSEL. BENJAMIN DAVIES, West Hoboken, N. J., assignor to L. Straus & Sons, New York, N. Y. Filed Mar. 20, 1895. Serial No. 542,546. Term of patent 7 years.

Reproduced from U.S. Patent Office files.

Flower center, signed with a star in circle
(L. Straus trademark), 12" in diameter.

PLATE 32

27. DAVIES', PATENTED JUNE 4, 1895

24,355. GLASS VESSEL. BENJAMIN DAVIES, West Hoboken, N. J., assignor to L. Straus & Sons, New York, N. Y. Filed Mar. 20, 1895. Serial No. 542,547. Term of patent 7 years.

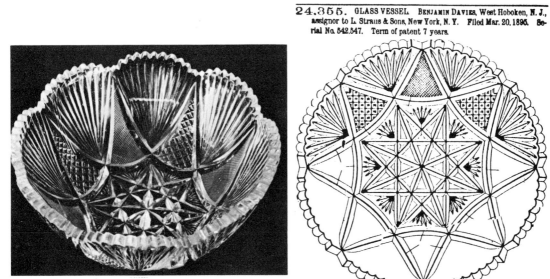

Patent 24355, Punch Bowl, 11½" diameter.

Reproduced from U.S. Patent Office files.

PLATE 33

28. IMPERIAL

"Imperial" was designed by William C. Anderson for the Libbey Glass Co. and patented June 4, 1895 #24356. It is a very desirable and scarce pattern, difficult to acquire.

Reproduced from U.S. Patent Office files.

Ice cream tray, patent #24356. Note adaptation of design to shape of tray.

PLATE 34

29. HARVARD

The pattern illustrated here contains three motifs: strawberry diamond hobnail, hobnail with a single star, and square with an "X" cut. This design is often confused with Russian which has only two elements, the pyramidal star and decorated or undecorated hobnail or "button."

The name "Harvard" was used by many glass houses for many patterns having no resemblance to each other. As used in this book, the design refers to the Harvard shown in a scrapbook of the Hawkes Co., and illustrated in Dorothy Daniels' book *Cut and Engraved Glass.*

8" tray with hobstar center; note scallops alternate star and strawberry diamond motifs.

Ice tub with matching plate, 6" tall to top of the tabs.

Plate 35

Bowling pin decanter, 16" tall, note shaped stopper in continuation of design.

Heart, 6" diameter, a very popular form in heavy demand for St. Valentine's day.

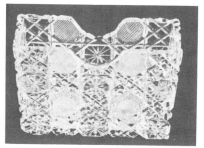

Holder for deck of cards.

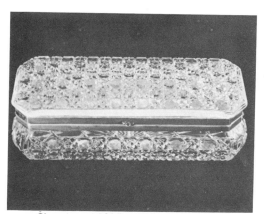

Glove box, 10¾" x 4" in choice overall cut.

Ship's decanter (note broad base,) used on boats, yachts, etc. 7¼" wide at base.

Plate 36

30. PRISM

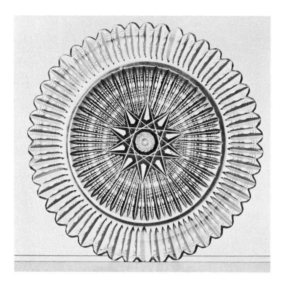

Plate 8½″ diam. all cut in prism except for hobstar center.

Stein with heavy sterling top, triple notched handle, 6″ tall, a very rare item in cut glass.

Plate 37

31. PRISM AND CHAIN (OF HOBSTARS)

Compote, 8″ tall with 24 point hobstar base.

6″ nappy reproduced from O. F. Egginton catalogue and titled "Prism."

Plate 38

32. PRISM AND BULLSEYE (BY A. SNOW, JR.)

Patented by A. Snow, Jr. for the Pairpoint Mfg. Co. (owner and operator of the Mt. Washington Glass Co. at New Bedford, Massachusetts).

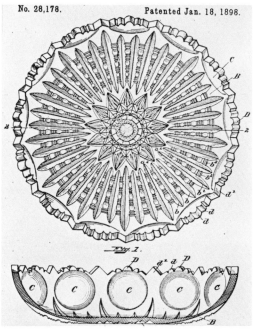

No. 28,178.   Patented Jan. 18, 1898.

Reproduced from U.S. Patent Office files.

#28282

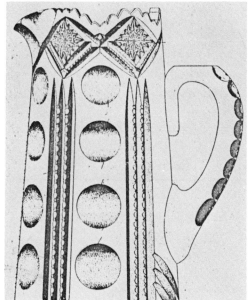

Reproduced from U.S. Patent Office files.

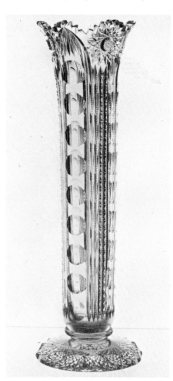

Vase, 16" tall in variation, 32 point hobstar base, hobstar and fan motifs added.

Prism and Bullseye (by Joseph Wilson)
Patented Feb. 15, 1898

Bowl 8¼" diameter in patent #28282

Plate 39

PRISM AND BULLSEYE

By Benj. Davies for L. Straus & Sons.
Pat. May 31, 1898   #28733

By Andrew Snow, Jr. for Mt. Washington
Glass Co.
Pat. Sept. 10, 1901   #35062

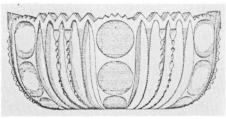

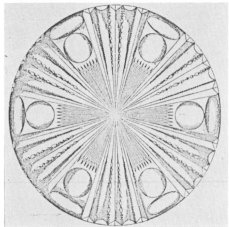

Reproduced from U.S. Patent Office files.

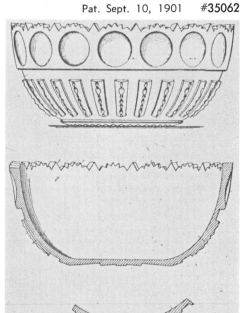

Reproduced from U.S. Patent Office files.

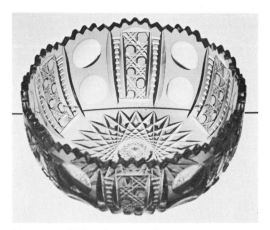

Variation: 8" bowl in emerald green cut to
clear, band of cane between vertical columns
of bead.

14" tall pitcher in variation, chain of hobstar
motif added.

Plate 40

33. BULLSEYE AND STAR

This is one of the most outstanding and beautiful designs of Joseph Wilson and of the Brilliant Period. It was patented Dec. 22, 1903.

Reproduced from U.S. Patent Office files.

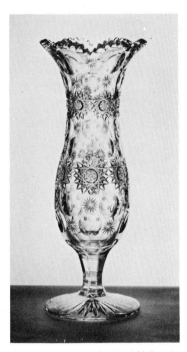

Pat. 36696, vase on a standard, 13½″ tall.

Plate 41

34. PUNTY AND RAISED DIAMOND (BY PAIRPOINT)

Reproduced from catalogue of the Pairpoint Corporation.

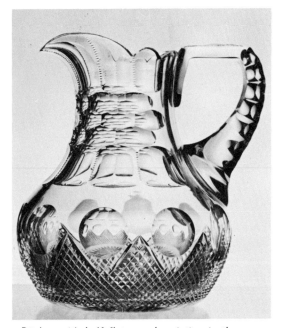

Pitcher with half flutes and variation in the raised diamond figure.

Plate 42

35. QUEENS

This pattern was cut by T. G. Hawkes & Co. on Steuben blanks that have never been surpassed for purity and beauty of color. The design, especially the bulls-eye motif as used, effectively mirrors and catches the refractions of light from every angle. It was popular and expensive. A Hawkes catalogue indicates a price of $315.00 for a dozen goblets. Any item in this pattern is a choice collector's item.

Rosebowl 7″ in diameter.

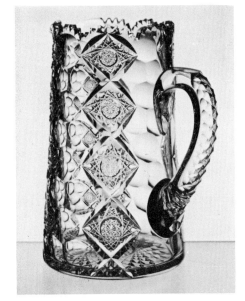

Pitcher, 8¾″ tall.

Tumbler, 3¾″ tall.

Signed Hawkes celery, 4¾″ x 11¼″, using the hobstar and bullseye in a variation.

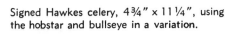

Plate 43

36. CRESWICK BY O. F. EGGINTON
Variation by J. Hoare

Note cross-hatched (strawberry diamond) triangle with rounded base motif and that the variation by J. Hoare uses the same motif with the prism motif added.

7" cheese dish, reproduced from O. F. Eggin-ton catalogue.

Tumble-up (carafe with matching tumbler that fits over the top of it) in J. Hoare design, but not signed.

Pitcher, 7½" high, signed J. Hoare, Corning, 1853.

8" bowl in J. Hoare pattern but not signed.

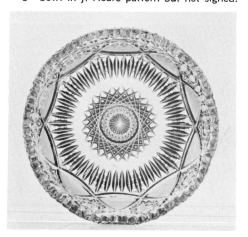

Plate 44

37 CORINTHIAN

L. Straus & Sons cut this design on fine quality blanks with deep and sharp cutting in the version illustrated below. It is an attractive and desirable pattern, collectible in sets because of the large amount made in this and related patterns of only minor variations. T. G. Hawkes & Co. cut a "Corinthian" that has cross cut diamond where the Straus design uses the cane motif (not illustrated). Other patterns called "Corinthian" were completely different.

Punch bowl, 12½" in diameter.

Oblong tray, 14" x 8½"

Cheese dish, plate 9", dome 6" in diameter.

Plate 45

38. ABERDEEN

After a detailed description in his patent papers, Thomas G. Hawkes names this design, patented April 14, 1896, "Aberdeen." Just how he arrived at the name is not known. It is a lovely, full-cut design. Comparatively little of it is available and pieces are collector's items.

8" low bowl in "Aberdeen"

#25386

Reproduced from U.S. Patent Office files.

39. "CLASSIC"

This rare and unique design by Thomas G. Hawkes is not typical of Brilliant Period designs. Its origin is often mistaken for foreign. Panels are laid out in which finely engraved flowers and figures appear. What is most unusual is the "fish scale" stippled type of background and the effective imitation of the genuine mined quartz rock crystal in the highly polished finish. It is unsurpassed in quality. The covered apothecary jar illustrated is majestic and formal. It embodies principles of design and beauty that are ageless. For these reasons, we call it "Classic."

Plate 46

Centerpiece bowl in "Classic", 10" in diameter at the top.

Covered apothecary jar 13¼" tall in "Classic."

40. VICTORIA

This design by Joseph B. Hill was patented December 15, 1896 and given patent #26396. He was the principal designer for the Imperial Cut Glass Co. of Philadelphia. For purposes of comparison, we include patent #26730 patented March 9, 1897 by Thomas G. Hawkes.

Reproduced from U.S. Patent Office files. #26730

#26396.   Reproduced from U.S. Patent Office files.

Plate 48

Note that both patterns have center radiants with figures between them. The Joseph B. Hill design alternates a strawberry diamond figure with hobstar and adds the fan motif to the outer chain.

Tray, approximately 13½" x 7" in variation of patent #26730 by Hawkes.

Decanter with sterling overlay stopper in variation of patent #26396.

Plate 49

41. FESTOON

This design, named "Festoon" in his patent papers #26731 by Thomas G. Hawkes was patented March 9, 1897. Basically, the central figure is an 8 point figure of two squares with large 24 point hobstar rosettes between the points.

Bowl, 8" diameter in "Festoon."

Reproduced from U.S. Patent Office files.

Plate 50

42. PINWHEEL (also known as "Buzz")

This pattern was patented February 28, 1899, #30267 by Patrick H. Healy for the American Cut Glass Co. of Chicago, Ill., a subsidiary of the Libbey Glass Co.

Much of the glass cut during the later part of the Brilliant Period reflects the attempt to reduce labor costs. This resulted in many pieces of inferior quality. The better pieces, however, are comparable to the best of the earlier patterns, are very desirable and well worth collecting.

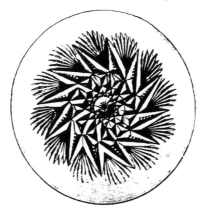

Small cream pitcher.

Plate 51

43. BAND OF STARS PATTERNS (including "Planeta" by L. Straus & Sons)

31,738. BOWL OR VESSEL. Benjamin Davies, West Hoboken, N. J., assignor to L. Straus & Sons. New York, N. Y. Filed Sept. 29, 1899. Serial No. 732,117. Term of patent 7 years.

"Planeta" design patented Oct. 31, 1899 by L. Straus & Sons.

Reproduced from U.S. Patent Office files.

Plate 52

"Planeta" by
L. Straus & Sons.

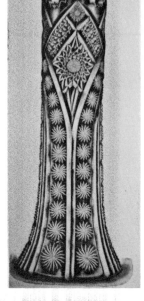

(Above) Bowl and tall vase reproduced from Glass & Crockery Journal.

9" Nappy with bands of stars and cane vesicas.

8" bowl with bands of stars, the four outside quarters alternate fan/notched prism with hobstar.

Plate 53

44. LILY OF THE VALLEY

This pattern, illustrated by objects of the Libbey Glass Co. was cut in slightly different ways by many other glass companies. It was one of the earlier "realistic" patterns.

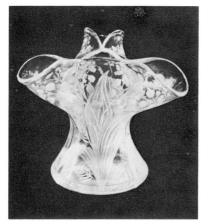

Tri-cornered centerpiece with folded corners signed "Libbey."

Bell, in design identical to Libbey pattern but not signed.

Plate 54

45. EULALIA (name from Higgins & Seiter catalogue)

Sugar and creamer. "Eulalia."

Oval salad, fruit, or berry bowl. "Eulalia."

Dish, 8½" square in "Eulalia" with arms of the cross in prism radiants. Note "shell" effect of scalloped fan corners.

Plate 55

46. "DRAPE" (L. Straus & Sons)

This design is described in the patent papers #35323 as having "curved banner effects." No pattern name appears but for purposes of reference we refer to it as the "Drape." It resembles a drape held back by two star tie-backs. It was designed by Herman Richman, Richmond, N.Y., and assigned to L. Straus & Sons. It was patented November 26, 1901. The cutting is excellent on fine quality glass and very attractive.

"Drape" flower centerpiece 12" diam.

Covered sugar and creamer, patent #35323

Reproduced from U.S. Patent Office files.

Two piece punch bowl in "Drape" 10" in diameter.

Plate 56

47. "DRAPE" BY LIBBEY GLASS CO.

This design by William Marrett was patented April 7, 1903 and assigned to the Libbey Glass Co. The pillar-festoons, the beading and the cross-hatched strawberry diamond represent the cut glass of the Brilliant Period at its very best. The quality of the glass itself is a connoisseur's delight. Anything in this pattern is a great rarity. For reference purposes, we call it Libbey's "Drape."

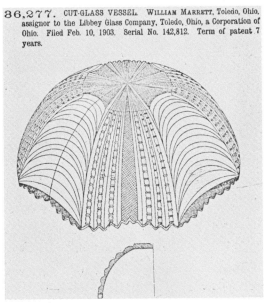

86,277. CUT-GLASS VESSEL. WILLIAM MARRETT, Toledo, Ohio, assignor to the Libbey Glass Company, Toledo, Ohio, a Corporation of Ohio. Filed Feb. 10, 1903. Serial No. 142,812. Term of patent 7 years.

Reproduced from U.S. Patent Office files.

Vase, 10" tall
patent #36277

Plate 57

48. "PINETREE" (our own name for identification)

Pitcher, 8" tall in "Pinetree."

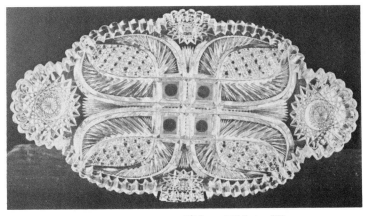

Ice cream tray, 16½" x 9¼" in "Pine-tree." Note four clear circles in the squares.

Plate 58

49. SENORA (from Libbey catalogue)

Reproduced from Libbey catalogue, 1904.

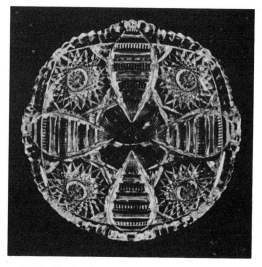

Bowl 9″ diameter in "Senora" pattern.

Plate 59

50. SOMERSET (from Libbey catalogue)

Bread tray with "balloon" shaped design similar to "Senora" (pattern 49 above), with fan and strawberry diamond motifs added 5″ x 11¾″.

"Somerset."
Reproduced from Libbey catalogue, 1904.

Plate 60

51. "EXPANDING STAR" (our name for reference)

This very sharp close cut design has exquisite detail and is always full cut. To us it suggests the expanding spray of a fireworks display. Both the glass and the execution of the design are of exceptional quality. Anything in this pattern is a fine addition to any collection.

Ice cream tray, 18 inches x 10 inches.

Four compartment dish, 8" diam. exclusive of handles.

Dish, 9" in diameter with large flat handles extending from the sides.

Plate 61

52. SPLIT VESICA AND BEAD

This pattern is one of the sharpest and most brilliant of the over-all cuts. The distinguishing feature (hence the name) is the vesica, split lengthwise by beading and the partitioning of the dish so that hobstar and the vesicas alternate around the central hobstar. Note the cross formed by the beading. The quality of the glass and cutting is superb and the design well balanced and integrated. Supply is very limited.

Carafe, 8¼″ tall.

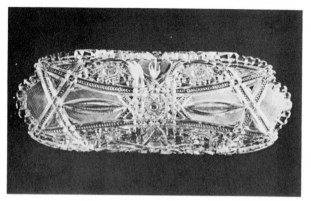

Celery dish, 11½″ x4″

Cheese dish, dome 6″, plate 9½″ in diameter.

Plate 62

53. LOTUS

This design by Walter Egginton patented February 24, 1903 #36233 was cut on the best quality Corning blanks by the O. F. Egginton Co. The catalogue of that firm lists the name of the pattern as "Lotus." The pieces cut in this design rate in category as "top of the grade" in beauty, brilliance and high craftsmanship. It is Egginton's best pattern always well executed. All of the pieces illustrated are signed with Egginton's trademark, a crescent and star.

Reproduced from U.S. Patent Office files.

Vase on a standard 13½" tall.

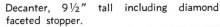

Decanter, 9½" tall including diamond faceted stopper.

Bowl, 8" in diameter.

Plate 63

54. "STALKS AND STARS"

This pattern design by William C. Anderson for the Libbey Glass Co. is well balanced and unique. No description is attempted or name given in the patent papers. The name "Stalks and Stars" is our own idea for reference purposes and calculated to help recall the design.

9 inch shallow bowl, pat. #38000.

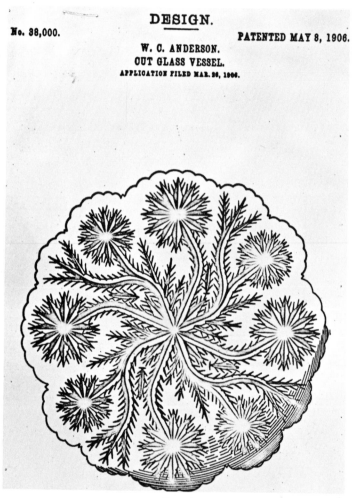

Reproduced from U.S. Patent Office files.

Fernbowl (has a clear liner) 7¾" diameter, pat. #38000.

Plate 64

55. SNOWFLAKE

This unique and brilliant design by Libbey is very rare. In the August 1961 issue of *Woman's Day* the name given for this pattern is "Snow-flake" and it is illustrated by a plate in the Toledo Museum of Art. The central motif does, of course, imitate the design of a snow crystal.

Oval tray, 11 5⁄8" x 7 3⁄4" signed "Libbey."

Plate 65

56. SPILLANE—SHELL TYPE

This beautiful design by D. F. Spillane was patented May 8, 1906, #38002 and cut by the Libbey Glass Co. The "X" cut vesicas and notched prism plus the use of the fan motif between the hobstars create the effect of a sea shell.

6 inch nappy, patent #38002

Reproduced from U.S. Patent Office files.

Plate 66

57. "OPEN PETAL" OR SHERWOOD

The "Open Petal" concept was named "Sherwood" in the catalogue of the O. F. Egginton Co. We think the design of Louis Hinsberger of Brooklyn, N.Y., patented May 19, 1908 patent #39313 is lovelier and has better detail. The general idea of the pattern was also cut by other glass houses with variations.

Reproduction of patent office copy.

Decanter, pat. #39313, 11 ¼" tall including diamond cut stopper.

Sherwood 8" bowl.
Reproduced from catalogue of the O. F. Egginton Co.

Low Bowl, 7 ½" diameter, cross split and fan motifs added.

Plate 67

58. WREATH AND FLOWER

Wreath and flower designs were cut by practically all the glass houses but most of them were either Hawkes or Sinclaire. Patent #39980 by Henry P. Sinclaire was patented August 3, 1909 and is typical. The photographs following are illustrations of some of the better designs by T. G. Hawkes & Co. All of the objects shown are signed pieces.

#39980

Reproduced from U.S. Patent Office files.

Teapot (very rare) signed "Hawkes," 10 inches wide from tip of spout to edge of handle.

Bowl, 9" in diameter signed "Hawkes," Note wreaths around the 8 point hobstar and the brilliant center star.

Round dish, 10" diameter with daisy, has applied green ribbon all around except for the center, design is cut through the ribbon, signed "Hawkes."

Plate 68

59. "LACE"

One of the outstanding patterns of the Hunt Glass Co. of Corning, N.Y., is the one pictured here which we call "Lace" for reference purposes. It presents a striking appearance, is expertly cut and the company blanks were usually from the Corning Glass Works or from the Steuben Glass Works. The principal motifs are chain of hobstars, panels with engraved flowers and a 32-point hobstar of exceptional brilliance. This desirable pattern was probably cut in only limited quantity.

Plate, 10¼" in diam. (not signed).

Rosebowl on 3 legs in "Lace" design, signed "Hunt," 7½" in diam. 6¼" high.

Plate 69

60. CORN AND RYE

Decanters, tumblers, highball glasses and pitchers were often made with deep intaglio cutting related to their intended use, generally for alcoholic beverages. They make a splendid addition to a cut glass collection.

Whiskey bottles appr. 14" tall including stoppers, Rye and Scotch thistle designs, signed Libbey.

Highball glass in "Corn" design, 4¾" tall, in Gravic Glass, signed Hawkes.

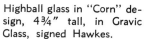

Plate 70

61. INTAGLIO DAISY, PATENTED MAY 11, 1909
62. CORNFLOWER, PATENTED JUNE 15, 1909

Patent 39982 by Albert Steffin for the Pairpoint Corp. and patent 40051 by Robert H. Pittman for T. B. Clark & Co. were among the first of the realistic designs cut in quantity. Worth while noting is the fact that excellent form and quality was still available in the blanks. Selection of the best pieces adds real value to a collection.

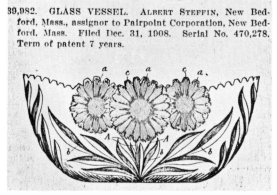

39,982. GLASS VESSEL. ALBERT STEFFIN, New Bedford, Mass., assignor to Pairpoint Corporation, New Bedford, Mass. Filed Dec. 31, 1908. Serial No. 470,278. Term of patent 7 years.

Reproduced from U.S. Patent Office files.

Pitcher on a standard, 13″ tall, intaglio daisy design with relief diamond motif added.

#40051

Reproduced from U.S. Patent Office files.

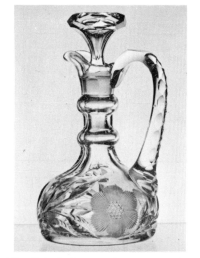

Cruet, 7″ tall including teardrop stopper, in cornflower pattern. Note enhancement of form by double ring and shape of handle.

Plate 71

63. BRUNSWICK

Brunswick is one of the designs by Thomas G. Hawkes that uses the simplicity of the pattern to enhance the beauty of glass (most likely Steuben) that has never been excelled for purity and quality of color. Basically, the motifs are chain of hobstars and clear flute panels separated by vertical lines of parallel line cutting. The desirability of objects in this design is obvious. The illustrations that follow are all signed with the Hawkes trademark.

Rosebowl on a standard 7" tall.

Tumbler and pitcher in "Brunswick."

Squat type pitcher.

Punch cup, appr. 3" diam.

Plate 72

64. BIRD-IN-THE-CAGE

This magnificent, fanciful pattern has the apt name "Bird-in-the-Cage" as appears evident on a look at the design with a little imagination. It is one of the best and most unusual of the Brilliant Period. The craftsmanship is of the highest order and although the design was cut in comparatively small quantity, collecting it is well worth the effort. It was patented Aug. 3, 1909 and assigned patent #40196.

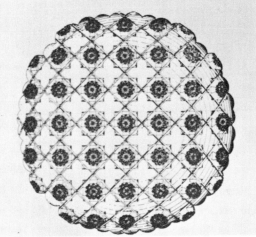

40,196. GLASS VESSEL OR SIMILAR ARTICLE. HENRY P. SINCLAIRE, Corning, N. Y., assignor to H. P. Sinclaire & Company, Corning, N. Y. Filed June 3, 1909. Serial No. 500,038. Term of patent 14 years.

Reproduced from U.S. Patent Office files.

Bowl, 7" diameter, in variation of patent #40,196.

Plate 73

65. "TRIPLE SQUARE"

The unique features of this design, patented August 10, 1909, #40213, by Thomas B. Clark, are the use of a square enclosed in two other squares, and the right angle serrated edge. A chain of hobstars is used around the piece. The design is distinctive and easily recognizable. Objects in this pattern are choice and very desirable.

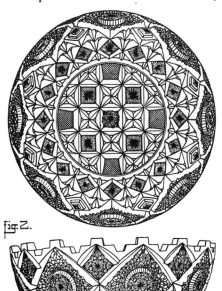

Fig. 2.

Reproduced from U.S. Patent Office files.

Pitcher 6¾" tall
Nappy, 7" in diameter

Plate 74

66. SHERATON

This unusual design by Thomas G. Hawkes is a fine example of triple mitre cutting in bands. It usually has either three or four medallions which are exquisitely engraved with baskets of flowers and cornucopias. A plate in this pattern was part of the T. G. Hawkes permanent display at the Smithsonian Institution, Washington, D.C. It represents Hawkes glass at its very best. Anything in this design, comparatively rare, is a highly desirable addition to an American cut glass collection.

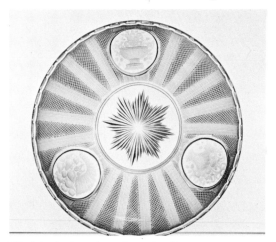

5" dish (enlarged to show detail).

Small tumbler on a standard 3¾" tall (very rare).

Bowl, 8" in diameter.

Small compote, top is 5¼" in diameter, honeycomb cut stem.

Plate 75

67. MILLICENT

This design is a Hawkes variation of the Sheraton. Small, delicate flowers are engraved between the fine line cutting. The heavily crosshatched bands are omitted. The glass is usually lighter in weight and not as deeply cut as the Sheraton. The over-all effect is very lovely and the pattern well worth collecting.

6" round box, knob of top in sterling overlay
(enlarged to show design).

12" vase with heavy sterling collar at top
(coll. of Martin J. Desmoni).

68. MEDALLION & DIAMOND (our name for reference)

This design of the H. P. Sinclaire Co. uses fine line cutting to create a sharp brilliance in the background. Sprays of flowers in arched panels and the use of clear diamond figures are distinctive features. Cut in this pattern were fingerbowls, plates and stemware. Note the use of elliptical "moons" or circles for border decoration. This is one of the most original and desirable of the Sinclaire designs.

Large, fluted compote, 12" in diameter,
9¼" high.

Goblet, 6¼" tall.

Plate 77

69. FERN

The use of step cutting to produce the fern motif creates a brilliant and beautiful result. The variations were cut by many glass houses. Some of these are illustrated here.

Jelly compote 8½″ tall with teardrop stem, fern and hobstar motifs.

Cordial bottle, 9″ tall including stopper, hobstar added to fern motif, no single stars.

This gracefully shaped pitcher on a standard, 14½″ tall, adds large hobstars to the fern and single star.

This exceptionally lovely pitcher with ornate hinged sterling top and cover was probably made on special order. 13½″ tall, motifs are fern and single star.

Plate 78

70. ROSEMERE (TUTHILL)

The illustrations of Tuthill intaglio glass on this and the following pages represent some of the finest intaglio cut glass ever made by any company. Unless otherwise stated, all bear the acid etched trademark.

Vase, 15½" tall with wide bands of deep cross hatching. Flowers and leaves have exquisite shading and detail.

Pitcher in unique shape with notched rim and cross-hatched band, 9" tall. Note how size and shape of the handle balance with form of body of pitcher.

Plate 79

71. WILD ROSE (TUTHILL)

This design is similar to Rosemere but without the crosshatched bands.

Goblet, 6¼" tall.

Perfume bottle, 5" in diameter with sterling

Plate 80

72. PRIMROSE (TUTHILL)

Compote 5" high, 8" in diameter at top, with the design also cut in the base.

Tumbler 3¾" tall, pitcher 9" high, part of a water set. Hobstar and strawberry diamond motifs added.

Plate 81

73. POPPY (TUTHILL)

74. PHLOX (TUTHILL)

Plate, 9⅝" in diameter with unique central figure and magnificent border in deep cut intaglio, fine example of "Poppy" design.

Flat plate in "Phlox" pattern, 7¾" in diameter. As in the "Poppy" plate at left, geometric motifs of hobstar and fan are used in the center figure in apposition to the intaglio work to enhance the general effect.

Plate 82

75. INTAGLIO GRAPE (also called "Vintage")

This pattern was cut by most of the glass houses but particularly by Tuthill, Hawkes, Sinclaire and Pairpoint.

Plate, 10", example of the finest intaglio in this pattern won first prize in the St. Louis World's Fair (1904) signed "Tuthill."

Basket signed "Tuthill," 10½" tall including handle, with chain of hobstars.

Pitcher in intaglio grape, reproduced from "Hawkes" catalogue.

Two handled bowl with design similar to Tuthill but with much less refinement in the detail, (signed "Sinclaire").

Plate 83

76. GREEK KEY

Greek Key was designed by Thomas A. Shanley and patented January 17, 1911, #41091. It was assigned to the International Silver Co. and cut by its subsidiary, the Meriden Cut Glass Co., Meriden, Conn.

Greek Key is incredibly brilliant, deep and close cut. Its central motif of hobstars and cane is offset by a simple wide Greek Key border and a right angle serrated edge. It was sold in the appropriate company of fine diamonds and gems in jewelers' shops. This exquisite design could only be executed on the highest quality blank. Being one of the most sought after patterns, even a single piece is a prize. It was often made with embellishments of sterling silver.

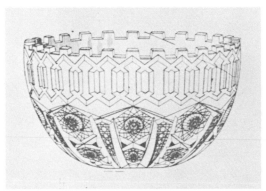

Reproduced from U.S. Patent Office files.

Plate, 10 inches in diameter.

Bread tray, 13" x 7", central motif appears almost like fine lace.

Low bowl, 8 inches in diameter.

Plate 84

77. HOLLY

Holly is one of the finest and most original of all the Henry P. Sinclaire designs. It was patented February 28, 1911, patent #41204. Its checkerboard pattern is deeply and sharply cut in tiny facets that must have taxed the craftsmen's skill to the utmost. The holly berries and leaves are well done and the general effect is one of great beauty. Objects in this pattern are rare and difficult to acquire.

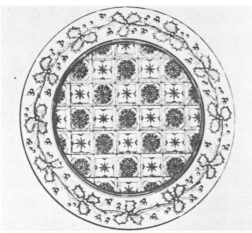

Reproduced from U.S. Patent Office files.

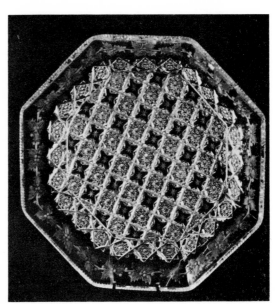

Octagon shaped tray, 10" in diameter, border in engraved holly, patent #41204, (signed "Sinclaire").

Signed "Sinclaire" pitcher, engraved holly border around top, hobstar base, triple notched handle. Note that the grouping of the leaves is not always in a group of three as called for by the patent.

Plate 85

78. COMET

"Halley's Comet" is named after the English astronomer who found that the paths of a certain comet observed in 1456, 1531 and 1607 were the same as the comet he saw in 1682. He had predicted that it would return to view about every 75 years. In expectation of its re-appearance in 1910 (which event did in fact occur), the idea of a comet pattern stirred the imagination of the designers. Illustrated here are the "Comet" designs of J. Hoare & Co., Tuthill and on Plate 114 the one by Libbey. All of them show originality and imagination. The quality of the glass and the cutting represents some of the best of the Brilliant Period. A collector would be fortunate to acquire any one of these beautiful patterns.

Ice tub, 7¾" diam. signed J. Hoare 1853, Corning.

Carafe, 8¼" tall signed J. Hoare, 1853, Corning.

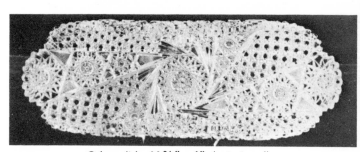

Celery dish, 11¾" x 4" (not signed).

8 inch bowl signed "Tuthill."

Plate 86

79. REX (by Tuthill Glass Co.)

It was a bowl in this design, exhibited at the Panama-Pacific Exposition in 1915 at San Francisco that won the first prize, a gold medal, for the finest piece entered into the competition. The pattern is well organized, its brilliance and perfection of cutting like a magnificent diamond. Mr. Harry Holmbraker, one of the most talented engravers in the country and formerly employed by the Tuthill Glass Co. told us, at the time of writing this book, that he believes many pieces were made in this pattern but because few collectors are willing to part with them, supply is very limited and prospects for purchase rather dim.

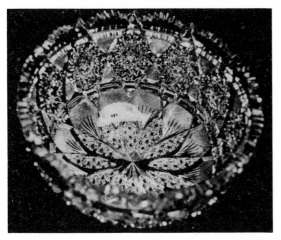

Celery dish, 13" x 5" in "Rex" pattern. (not signed).

Bowl in "Rex," collection of Doris (Mrs. Frank Powell), daughter of Charles G. and Jennie Burt Tuthill. (not signed).

Plate 87

80. ROYAL

This design by Harry S. Hunt was patented July 11, 1911 #41555. The center or bottom cutting looks like the Russian pattern but a closer examination shows the hobstar button with 12 facets around it instead of the usual six or eight. It is cut deeply and fully and one of the best of the Hunt Glass Co. line.

8 inch bowl, patent #41555

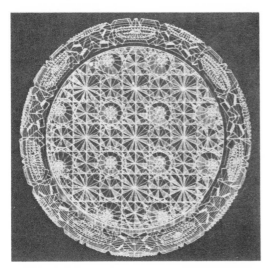

Reproduced from U.S. Patent Office files.

Plate 88

81. FLUTES AND HOBSTAR (CHAIN) PATENT #42333

82. FLUTES AND HOBNAIL (CHAIN) PATENT #42334

These designs by Henry R. Luckock and Charles H. Taylor were patented March 19, 1912, and assigned to the Jewel Cut Glass Co. of Newark, N.J. This company's name does not loom prominently among the cut glass houses of the Brilliant Period but these two patterns belie any lack of stature as to the excellence of their product. It is very much to their credit that these patterns which must have been very expensive to produce, should be attempted at a time when the cheaper pressed cuts were being made in competition. The glass is of the best Steuben crystal clear quality and the deep close cutting a lapidary's delight. The patterns are similar except that in the Flutes and Hobnail design #42334, a band of tiny, sharp hobnails is substituted for the circle chain of hobstars in patent #42333. Anything in either of these patterns belongs in the category—the best of cut glass.

42,333.   Patented Mar. 19, 1912.

Reproduced from U.S. Patent Office files.

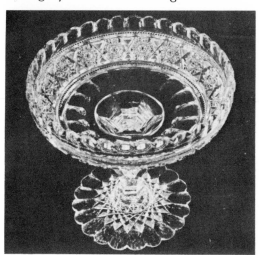

Large compote, 8" in diameter with knobbed teardrop stem, pat. #42333.

10 inch tray plus a wide (2") sterling band around the rim of it, pat. #42334

#42334

Reproduced from U.S. Patent Office files.

Plate 89

83. BASKET, BY FRY (patented Feb. 20, 1917)

50,334. GLASS ARTICLE. FRED L. ANDREWS, Beaver, Pa., assignor to H. C. Fry Glass Company, Rochester, Pa., a Corporation of Pennsylvania. Filed Aug. 2, 1916. Serial No. 112,858. Term of patent 14 years.

Reproduced from U.S. Patent Office files.

7" plate signed "Fry" patent number 50334. Border of radiants has been added to original patent design.

Plate 90

84. ROOSTER

The trend toward realism reached into the barnyard. Three panels of hobstar, strawberry diamond and fan alternate with three sections having deep intaglio cut roosters with fine detail. Execution of the design and quality of the glass is excellent.

Plate 91

85. ARCADIA

The catalogue of the Sterling Glass Co. of Cincinnati, Ohio, lists the pattern of the sugar and creamer below as "Arcadia." The use of the five sided strawberry diamond figure with the hobstar was common with many companies. In the Arcadia, the single star motif is added. Pieces in this pattern are usually fully cut and of fine quality.

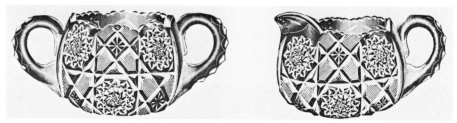

Reproduced from catalogue of the Sterling Glass Co.

Sugar and creamer on a standard, appr. 5" tall in variation, cane and fan being added and star motif omitted.

Punch bowl on a separate **standard**, 13½" in diameter in "Arcadia."

Plate 92

86. BUTTERFLY

Butterflies, with flowers or plants often added, were favorite subjects of the cut glass designers. Examples of the finest intaglio work with this attractive motif are illustrated below.

Plate 9⅝" in diameter signed Tuthill in butterfly and primrose, of rare beauty and quality.

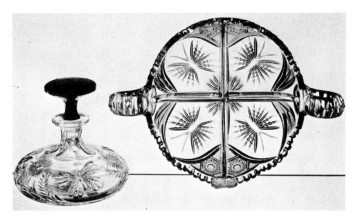

Perfume bottle and four part dish, 7" in diameter by Tuthill (but only perfume bottle signed).

BUTTERFLY AND THISTLE

Flared vase, 7" in diameter, note notched rim.

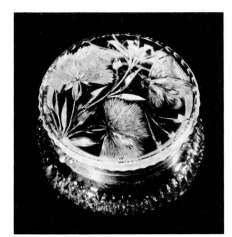

Round hinged box 5" in diam.

Plate 93

87. URN WITH FLAME BY FLOYD F. CARY
for the Pairpoint Corp. patented April 3, 1917

88. URN WITH DAISY BY HERMAN RICHMAN
for L. Straus & Sons, patented July 10, 1917

These patterns by different designers bear striking similarities. Both have heavy bands of cross-hatching and use the flute motif around a central figure. The center designs, however, are different, and the Straus pattern has a daisy placed between the leaves.

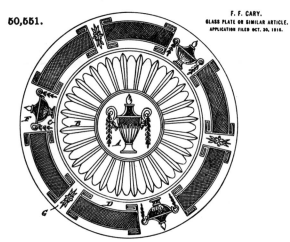

50,551.

F. F. CARY.
GLASS PLATE OR SIMILAR ARTICLE.
APPLICATION FILED OCT. 30, 1916.

Reproduced from U.S. Patent Office files.

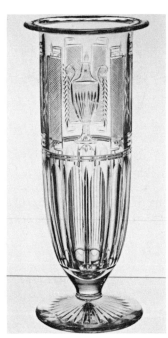

Vase 12" tall, pat. #50551 by the Pairpoint Corp.

H. RICHMAN.
GLASS ARTICLE.
APPLICATION FILED MAY 5, 1917.

51,028.   Patented July 10, 1917.

Reproduced from U.S. Patent Office files.

Bowl, 9" in diameter, pat. #51028 by L. Straus & Sons.

Plate 94

89. REGAL

Regal compote, height 8".

Regal vase.

(reproduced from the catalogue of the Sterling Cut Glass Co. Cincinnati, Ohio.)

Plate 95

90. STERLING

This pattern was given the company name.

Sterling Puff Box   Sterling Hair Receiver   Sterling Cologne

(reproduced from the catalogue of the Sterling Cut Glass Co.)

Plate 96

91. BERRY PATTERNS

Intaglio cut berry designs of real merit were cut by many companies. A few are here illustrated.

7-in. Plate. Raspberry.
Reproduced from Fry catalogue

Strawberry plate signed Sinclaire, 7" diameter.

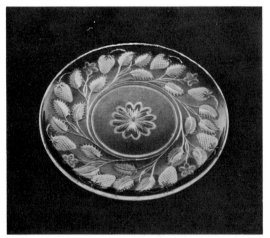

Strawberry plate, 9" in diam.

Blackberry plate 7¾" signed Tuthill.

Plate 97

92. GLENWOOD

93 PREMIER

94. NEWPORT

95. LOTUS

Reproduced from the *Glass and Crockery Journal* (about 1897) are examples of four of the patterns of J. D. Bergen Co., Meriden, Conn. The designs, by Bergen himself, were sharp cut on good quality blanks. They are illustrated here for reference purposes but they are not the type easily recognized or remembered.

Flower Centre, "Glenwood." Made in 8, 10 and 12 in. sizes.

"Premier" Ice tub and plate.

Qt. Carafe, "Newport."

"Premier" Goblet. Also made in entire line of stemware.

Bonbon, "Lotus."

Plate 98

UNUSUAL PATTERNS (NOT OTHERWISE IDENTIFIED)

Tray, 14½" x 8¼" with wide cane bands.

Dish, "shell" type, 8" diam.

Large cheese dish, plate 10½" diam. dome
7", in hobstar and strawberry diamond with
beading around vesicas.

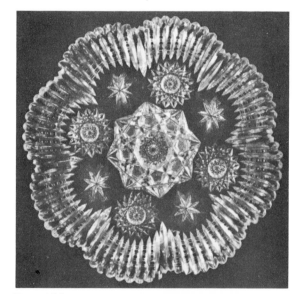

Tray, 12" in diameter with brilliant combination of hobstar, flashed star and prism.

Plate 99

UNUSUAL PATTERNS (NOT OTHERWISE IDENTIFIED)

6¾" plate in strawberry diamond, hobstar, fan and cane vesicas.

10" plate with wide border of very fine line cutting, hobstar, cane and "X" motifs.

8" dish, 13 hobstars in center with single stars around and chains of flutes.

Cheese and cracker dish with one inch sterling rim reticulated. The center (with flashed single star) raised for placement of cheese, lower part for crackers.

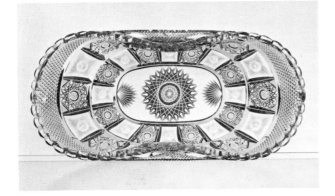

Bread tray 11¾" x 5½", top and bottom sides turn inward, in very rare and unique design.

Plate 100

EXAMPLES OF EARLY AND MIDDLE PERIOD

Left: Decanter 16″ tall, flute and grape motifs, similar to one engraved by A. Jardel and presented to James Monroe by Benjamin Bakewell in 1817.

Right: Pitcher, rare and probably special order, of early American Period, 12″ tall, heavy sterling top with relief decoration. The heavy relief diamond and strawberry diamond squares suggest that it is either Boston and Sandwich Glass Co. or the New England Glass Co.

Sugar, olive dish and covered jar in motifs typical of Early Period.

Left: Decanter with cross-hatched arched pillars, small strawberry diamond cut squares and swirl, suggest it probably is from Stourbridge Flint Glass Works, Pittsburgh, Penna.
Right: Celery vase typical of Dorflinger, circa 1860.

Plate 101

T. B. CLARK & CO. INC., HONESDALE, PENNA.

The T. B. Clark company bought out the Maple City Glass Co. in 1904 and much of the output of both companies was in standard patterns on good quality blanks. Illustrated below are some of their better designs not previously shown. All of the pieces here are signed with the "Clark" trademark.

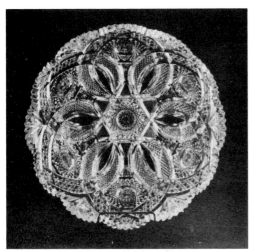

10½" bowl with clear vesicas surrounded by tiny, sharp hobnail.

Pitcher 9½" high, chain of hobstars, prism and notched prism motifs.

Bowl, 8¼" diam. with 32 point hobstar surrounded by small sharp hobnail.

Dish, of unique design, 9¾" partitioned into 3 sections by cane and hobstar radiants.

Plate 102

DORFLINGER: Long Island Flint Works 1852-1863
                       Greenpoint Glass Works 1860-1863
                       Wayne County Glass Work (White Mills, Pa. 1865-1881)
                       C. Dorflinger & Sons, 1881-1921

Christian Dorflinger was born in Alsace, France, on March 16, 1828. When only 18, he came to the United States with his widowed mother, brothers and sisters. Prior to his arrival he had spent eight years learning his trade from an uncle, a glassworker in St. Louis, Lorraine (France).

When a glass plant was established in Brooklyn to manufacture lamp shades and chimneys for kerosene lamps, he was chosen to manage it and in 1852 he moved to Brooklyn to be nearby. The business thrived and in 1858 he bought out the interest of Captain Flower and his associates, the original owners.

In 1860 Dorflinger established the Greenpoint Glass Works on Commercial Street in Brooklyn. A set of glassware which Mrs. Lincoln selected the following year for state occasions at the White House was made here and used until Grover Cleveland chose the newer Russian pattern of the Hawkes company. President Harrison acquired a set of 520 pieces in the Russian design for $6,000 from this plant. Theodore Roosevelt ordered the first highball glasses. Special commissions for elaborately designed glass to be used on the largest private yachts were given by the Vanderbilts, Goulds and Reids. One for Harry Clay Pierce was valued at $60,000.

Ill health brought on by over-exertion and strain compelled him to retire in 1863. After two years of recuperation Dorflinger decided to re-enter the glass business. By the fall of 1865 he had constructed a five pot furnace at White Mills, Penna., where he had previously purchased a farm for his retirement. Highly skilled men from Europe and employees from his Greenpoint factory were brought in to train local workers. By 1873 this plant, called the Wayne County Glass Works, was so successful he decided to concentrate his attention there.

The name of the business at White Mills continued unchanged until his sons William, Louis and Charles were made partners in 1881 and the firm name became C. Dorflinger and Sons. Eventually, the glass works became one of the largest in this country and Dorflinger cut and engraved glass became known the world over for its excellence of quality, beauty and design. By 1903 over 650 persons were employed by the plant and it consisted of 27 buildings. Glass blanks were supplied to 22 cutting shops in Wayne County alone in addition to those produced for their own use.

Among the prominent men employed at various times were Ralph Barber, Nicholas Lutz (later known for his Venetian-type striped glass),

Charles Northwood and the Larsen Brothers. One of his outstanding cutters and designers was John S. O'Connor, Jr., foreman of the cutting shop.

Christian Dorflinger died in 1915 at the age of 87. His sons carried on the business until 1921.

Dorflinger glass did not use an acid-etched trademark. Instead paper stickers were attached to each piece. Unfortunately, this has made authentication later on more difficult. Where silver was used in conjunction with his cut glass, the name "Dorflinger" was often imprinted on the metal.

Designs in this book designated "Dorflinger" are identified from patent papers (e.g. "Parisian" and "Middlesex") and from authenticated pieces of the Brooklyn Museum. Others are illustrated in Dorflinger catalogues and publications. His cased glass in green cut to clear was exceptionally fine in the depth and brilliance of its color. Although more plentiful than other colors made such as blue, topaz and chartreuse, any piece of Dorflinger, clear or colored is comparatively rare and worthy of a collector's cabinet space.

DORFLINGER PATTERNS

Pitcher circa 1897, in cross cut diamond, strawberry diamond and fan motifs with upper part in clear panels and notching (courtesy of the Brooklyn Museum).

Vase, flaring serrated rim, with hobstar, bullseye and notching, made at White Mills, Pa., part of a wedding set made for his daughter Carlotta Dorflinger 1897, (courtesy of the Brooklyn Museum).

Claret glass, water tumbler and sherry glass in Dorflinger's variation of "Middlesex" pattern, (courtesy of The Brooklyn Museum).

Pitcher on a standard in exquisitely graceful form in honeycomb pattern, with unique type of handle, circa 1852 (courtesy the Corning Museum of Glass).

Plate 103

DORFLINGER PATTERNS

Milk pitcher made at the Dorflinger factory, White Mills, Pa. 1874 (courtesy of the Brooklyn Museum)

Vase, flint glass made as a presentation piece for Mrs. Dorflinger and presented to her January 14, 1859 (courtesy of the Brooklyn Museum)

Punch bowl

Banquet lamp

Decanter

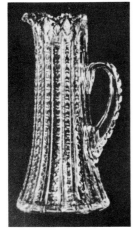

Tall jug

Berry bowl with "Rock Crystal" band.

Goblet in "Rock Crystal."

Plate 104

H. C. FRY GLASS CO.
ROCHESTER, PENNA. (1900-1929)

Henry Clay Fry as early as November 3, 1868 secured the first patent for a cut glass design (illustrated below). His own glass factory, however, was not established in Rochester, Pennsylvania, until 1900.

While employed by the William Phillips Glass Co. of Pittsburgh, he is said to have influenced President Lincoln in his promotion of American cut glass for export to other countries.

Fry was a leader in the cut glass industry during the "Middle Period" (1830-1880) and continuing into the "Brilliant Period." His hand-made blanks were unusual in shape. At its best, Fry glass was superb in its clarity and color; the cutting was sharp and precise; designs were original in conception.

The entry of Fry and others into the manufacture of pressed wares and more "commercial" items (such as heat resistant glass for baking, etc.) coincided with and followed the decline of the cut glass industry. His factory continued in operation until 1929. A simple acid-etched signature "Fry" was the usual trademark used to identify his early products.

Later pieces show deterioration in the quality of the blanks used, the cutting and in overornamentation.

In buying Fry cut glass, one should judge the specific merits of the particular item rather than depend on the signature or a generalization as to the quality of the over-all production.

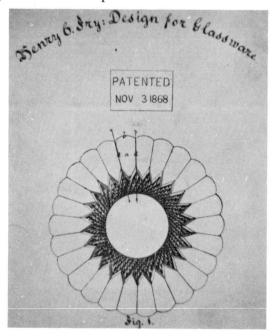

Plate 105

FRY SIGNED PIECES

Right: One of the largest composite pieces of American cut glass ever made, consisting of a punch bowl 18″ in diam., a five part pedestal and 12 footed punch glasses in the Rochester pattern. Made by the H. C. Fry Co. in 1905, height 4½ feet, weight appr. 150 lbs., formerly owned by the Carnegie Institute of Pittsburgh, Pa.

Deep bowl, 9½″ in diam. in close cut design with effect of elegant lace.

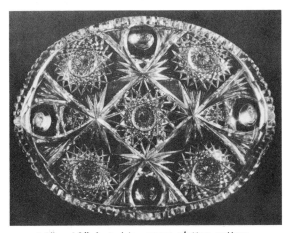

14″ x 10″ footed ice cream platter, pattern listed in Fry catalogue as "Sciota."

Right: 7½″ triangle shape fern dish, listed in Fry catalogue as "Frederick" pattern.

Plate 106

T. G. HAWKES GLASS CO. (1880-1890)
T. G. HAWKES & CO. (1890-1962)

Note: Steuben Glass Co. was a subsidiary of the Hawkes Co. from 1903 to 1918.

The T. G. Hawkes Glass Company was founded in 1880 by Thomas G. Hawkes whose family, of Irish and English descent had been engaged in the manufacture and cutting of glass for five generations. Before opening his own shop, he was a cutter for the J. Hoare Co. at first in Brooklyn and later in Corning, New York. In 1863 he came to Brooklyn and pursued his trade there until 1880 when he established a shop in Corning, cutting and engraving glass blanks of the Corning Glass Co.

About 1890, O. F. Egginton and H. P. Sinclaire, Jr., both of Corning, New York, became partners of Hawkes and the name of the firm was then changed to T. G. Hawkes & Co. The trademark of two hawks in a trefoiled ring came into use after July 1, 1890.

In 1903, Hawkes, his son Samuel and Frederick Carder of Stourbridge, England, formed the Steuben Glass Company as a subsidiary of the Hawkes Co. From that time on until the Steuben Co. was sold to the Corning Glass Co. in 1918, only Steuben blanks were used. Thereafter Hawkes was compelled to look elsewhere for his blanks. The decline in their over-all quality plus other factors forced the Hawkes factory to close in 1962.

In judging the quality of a Hawkes piece a great deal depends on the quality of the blank. The acid-etched trademark on late pieces is no guarantee of high quality. The boast of the Hawkes Co. that "pressed" blanks were never used was true at least until 1918. Recently some pressed pieces with inferior cutting, probably very late, have shown up with the acid-etched signature.

Hawkes glass at its best is magnificent and unsurpassed, especially when cut on Corning blanks or the blanks of the Steuben Co. Hawkes himself personally originated and patented some of the best designs of the "Brilliant Period." They were often refreshingly different and better. In addition Hawkes glass was expertly and deeply cut in the best of taste. Little of it is "run-of-the-mill." The variety and versatility of Hawkes during the period of more than 80 years the firm was in existence covered a very wide range.

The company received many well deserved honors. The "Grecian" and the "Chrysanthemum" patterns won the grand prize at the Paris Exposition in 1889. These patterns are rare and much sought after today by collectors. Even a single piece is a treasure to be hoarded. Hawkes glass also won high honors at the Chicago World's Fair in 1893 and at the St. Louis Exposition in 1904. In 1885 President Grover Cleveland ordered fifty dozen pieces in the Russian pattern for the White House, each piece bearing the U.S. Coat of

Arms. During the early 1900's orders for Hawkes glass came from W. H. Vanderbilt, John Jacob Astor, Joseph Chamberlain, Chauncey M. DePew, Charles M. Schwab and later from Franklin D. Roosevelt.

The Hawkes company is also known for its deeply cut intaglio glass it named "Gravic." The registration of the trademark filed January 7, 1903 reads: "The word GRAVIC. Used since December 13, 1902." "Iris," "Fruit" and "Carnation" are illustrated in this book as examples of this type of cutting. The finest pieces, deep cut with soft and detailed nuances in the gray unpolished surfaces represent some of the best intaglio work American craftsmen ever produced. Later work was not as deep and showed much less refinement in the execution of detail. In some instances, the piece was fully polished as in their "rock crystal" or "copper engraved" work in which Hawkes excelled. Not all pieces of Hawkes "Gravic" are signed. The earlier ones were more likely to be marked with the Hawkes trademark of two hawks in a shamrock either with or without the additional words "Gravic Glass."

Any Hawkes "Gravic Glass" is a very desirable collector's item. Comparatively little of it was made as it involved high labor costs.

HAWKES SIGNED GLASS

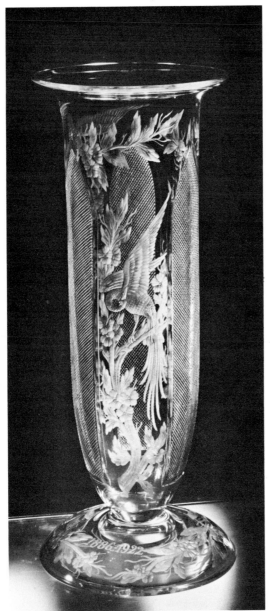

Jack-in-the-pulpit, rare, Hawkes glass at its best, 12" tall, top in sharp relief diamond with fan at the point, neck in Saint Louis diamond (also called concave diamond or honeycomb), balance in hobstars, strawberry diamond and fan.

This unusual, rare example of Hawkes' superb engraving, a vase 12" tall, was made as a commemorative piece "1886-1922." The sharp cross-hatched vertical panels frame a picture of a large bird with its wings spread and the plumage of its long tail hanging down amidst delicate flowers and leaves.

Plate 107

HAWKES "GRAVIC" INTAGLIO GLASS

Bucket shaped vase, with sterling base, height 8½", in "Iris" pattern.

Jewel box, 6½" square, with convex shaped top, in "Iris" pattern.

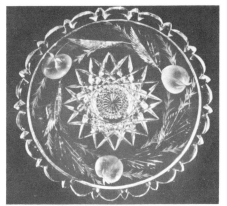

7" nappy in "Fruit" design.

Compote 6¼" diam. hobstar base, "Fruit" design.

Rosebowl on three legs approx. 6¼" diameter. "Carnation" pattern.

Plate, 11" diam. with nuances of rare quality, in "Carnation" pattern.

Plate 108

HAWKES SIGNED PIECES

8″ dish in one of Hawkes' most brilliant patterns.

Pitcher 9″ tall with flute panel around top, balance in hobstar, fan, bullseye, ladder (step cut) motifs.

Basket with heavy sterling rim and handle, cut and engraved, 6″ in diameter.

Pitcher, height 9½″ in hobstar, cross-cut diamond and fan.

Four compartment dish, octagon shaped, 7½″ diameter, 1½″ gallery cut with chain of hobstars, base has finely engraved flowers and ferns.

Plate 109

HAWKES SIGNED GLASS

Epergne in a simple design of great elegance. In two pieces, the center tray, 8″ in diam., has a stem that fits into the holder of the bottom tray which is 14″ wide. Note overlap rim on lower tray which has a giant 40 point hobstar. Motifs are chain of hobstars, fan and cross cut diamond.

Octagon shaped dish 8½″ in diam., 32 point hobstar center with engraved leaf border.

Flower center 6″ high, 7″ diameter, panel flutes, bullseye and fan motifs, hobstar base.

Plate 110

HAWKES CUT GLASS

Goblet, "An example of Hawkes Rock Crystal" (reproduced from Hawkes catalogue)

Relish dish, oblong, 4" x 8" with triple mitre fine line cutting, hobstars and fans.

Vase, "an example of Hawkes Gravic Glass" (reproduced from Hawkes catalogue)

Fern bowl, 8½" diam. on 3 triple claw legs, simple borders around rim in sharp contrast to brilliant center star of radiants.

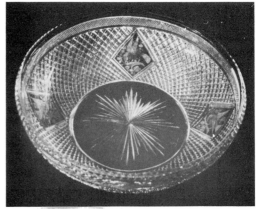

Dish, 8" in diam. with engraved birds in 4 diamond shaped fields surrounded by deep cross cut diamond, finely cross hatched band near rim.

Plate 111

J. HOARE & CO.

J. Hoare & Co., originally known as Hoare, Burns and Dailey, moved their business in 1863 from their South Ferry Works in New York to the Greenpoint Flint Glass Works (from which Christian Dorflinger then retired). In 1873 the site of their operations was changed to Corning, New York. Blanks of the Corning Glass Co. were used in their extensive cutting activities. The designers and craftsmen of the J. Hoare company were among the best of that time. Illustrated below are examples authenticated by the acid-etched signature and trademark "J. Hoare & Co. 1853, Corning."

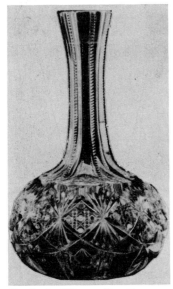

10" plate in unique design center Greek cross is in sharpest "Russian" (clear button), 4 medallions, 2 with wreaths, 2 with vases and flowers, finest cross-hatched strawberry diamond bands, very rare, probably for special use.

Carafe in "Croesus" pattern, an expensive design cut in limited quantity, exclusive with J. Hoare & Co.

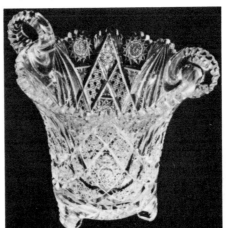

Deep bowl, 10" diam. with teardrop and notched prism radiants, hobstar and fan.

Plate 112

Footed ice bucket with notched handles, 7½" diam. at top exclusive of handles, bands of cane, and motifs of hobstar, strawberry diamond and stars.

J. HOARE & CO. SIGNED PIECES

Pitcher, 9″ tall, vesicas with clear split against a strawberry diamond background, also hobstar and fan motifs.

Vase, 12½″ high, 4″ in diam., vertical panels of hobstar and notched prism.

Dish, 6″ in diam. in unusual design, "shell" type.

Bread tray, 13″ x 6″, with extended handles, hobstar, strawberry diamond, cane and star motifs.

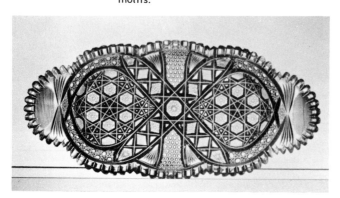

PLATE 113

LIBBEY:

New England Glass Co. South Boston, Mass. 1818-1878
New England Glass Co., W. L. Libbey & Sons, 1880-1888
New England Glass Co., W. L. Libbey & Son, 1880-1888
W. L. Libbey & Son, 1888-1893 (Toledo, Ohio)
Libbey Glass Co., Toledo, Ohio, 1893-

In 1812 a group of workers established themselves at East Cambridge, Mass., under the name "Porcelain & Glass Manufacturing Co." The enterprise did not succeed and the company was sold at auction to the New England Glass Co. incorporated under the laws of the State of Massachusetts. Established in 1818 the glassworks included "Two flint glass furnaces and twenty-four glass cutting mills, operated by steam, and a red lead furnace; capable of making two tons of red lead per week, (it) enabled them to produce every variety of fine, plain, mold and the richest cut-glass, . ."

The New England Glass Co. passed into the control of William L. Libbey in 1878. For many years previous, he had acted as their agent. Edward D. Libbey, his son, was made a member of the firm in 1880 and when his father died in 1883, responsibility for the business passed to him.

Recognizing the advantages that low cost natural gas would bring, E. D. Libbey moved the factories in 1888 to Toledo, Ohio. The better control of temperature through the use of gas made possible high quality glass of uniform color.

Libbey glass is usually heavy and deeply cut. Most of their designs were original and protected by patent. A large number of their patterns were the creations of the talented and resourceful William C. Anderson. Among some of the patterns illustrated in this book for which he was responsible were: "Middlesex," "Florence," "Stratford," "Wedgemere," "Kimberly," "Columbia," "Imperial" and "Stalks and Stars." Two outstanding designs (not by Anderson) were the brilliant "Comet" and "Drape."

Libbey never used pressed blanks. During the many years that Libbey cut glass the blanks were always of excellent color and crystal purity with execution of the patterns by the finest craftsmen. Libbey also made intaglio cut glass of exceptional merit.

Joseph Locke during his employment with Libbey invented Amberina (1883) Pomona (1885), Peachblow and Agata, all of which helped the fortunes of the company at a time it was running a loss on its over-all business.

Most of the larger pieces after 1895 were signed with the acid-etched trademark. With very few exceptions, Libbey cut and engraved glass is a most desirable addition to any collection.

12 inch tray in Libbey's Comet pattern (signed)

Plate 114

LIBBEY SIGNED PIECES

Pitcher in deeply carved intaglio fruit and leaves.

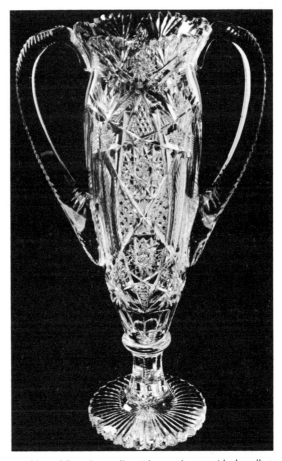

Vase 18 inches tall, with two large wide handles, base is cut in deeply ridged radiants.

"Lovebirds," a "painting" in deep intaglio on purest crystal, top of pitcher has sharp cross-hatched band.

Plate 115

LIBBEY SIGNED PIECES

Tray 12" diam. cut in tiny sharp hobnail with clear borders around the vesicas.

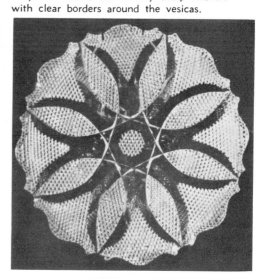

12" plate in unique pattern, the fluted scallops and bands enhance the beauty of the liquid clear quality of the glass.

Dish, 9" diam. in a simple, well organized design with fine line cutting and cross hatching in center.

Bowl with large overlap brim, 9" in diameter; sometimes this shape is referred to as "Bishop's hat."

Plate 116

LIBBEY SIGNED GLASS

Tray, approximately 12″ in diameter, large hobstar rosettes separated by 6 pointed star, large "Y" in center with brilliant flashings.

Vase, height 9¾″, top part in clear flute with rays, center section flashed stars and fine line cutting, chain of ovals and splits around bottom near base.

Heart shaped dish, 10″ at widest part, center with hobnail points, fine line cutting in shape of leaf, criss-crossed border near edge.

LIBBEY SIGNED GLASS

Deep, tri-cornered dish with three sides turned in, 9½" in diameter, hobstar, cane and fan motifs.

Butter dish in hobstar, cane and notched prism, plate 8", dome 5¼" diameter.

Bread tray with center cross in strawberry diamond, remainder of piece in sharp notched prism and hobstars.

Plate 118

H. P. SINCLAIRE & CO. (1904-1929)

At a time when many glass cutting houses were going out of business because of the prohibitive costs of labor and materials, Henry Purdon Sinclaire on May 14, 1904, announced the incorporation of the H. P. Sinclaire Co., "producers of cut and engraved glass of the highest quality." His family background adequately and fortuitously prepared him for his later accomplishments.

Sinclaire, a member of a prominent family had shortly before resigned as vice-president and secretary of the T. G. Hawkes Co. Undoubtedly, his association with this outstanding company and with his father, who was one of the original stockholders of the Corning Glass Works, contributed valuable knowledge and experience. His brother, the late William Sinclaire, was secretary of the Corning Glass Works. The Sinclaires were related to the Houghton family (founders of the Corning glassworks) by marriage a few generations back.

The Sinclaire factory, 60 feet wide and 120 feet long, was completed about September 1904 and employed about 200 workers. Marvin Olcott, Sr. was the principal other investor and became vice-president of the company. There were 12 other cut glass factories located in the city at the time. The factory manufactured no glass but purchased blanks elsewhere, usually from the Corning Glass Works, then cut and engraved the blanks.

The work of this company was of high quality and included many worthwhile original designs and forms by Sinclaire personally. The sharpness and closeness of the cutting in patterns such as "Holly," "Bird-in-the-cage," and "Medallion and Diamond" illustrated in this book are a marvel of high craftsmanship. Later pieces, in an effort to cut labor costs, left larger areas uncut, yet achieved beautifully simple, integrated designs that did not diminish the artistic result. In fact, the brilliance and quality of the glass were often accentuated by the clear areas of the glass. Deep intaglio cutting was often combined with geometrical designs and finely engraved work. Sinclaire's love of nature and feeling for flowers and fruit was often reflected in some of the finest intaglio work ever done.

Many of the Sinclaire pieces included borders of round or elliptically shaped "moons," clear fluting and panels formed by notched lines, and the frequent use of engraved flowers and leaves within panels or ovals. The inclusion of chains of hobstars in diamond shaped fields (a motif also used by many others) was often repeated. Patterns were generally simple, balanced and clearly conceived, never a conglomeration of too many motifs.

All of the pieces illustrated are signed (acid-etched) with the word "Sinclaire" or the "S" in the wreath providing reasonably authentic proof of their origin as the work of the Sinclaire factory. In addition, patent dates and numbers are given when known.

Some time after the death of H. P. Sinclaire in June of 1927, the Corning plant was sold to the Cobakco Co. by the Sinclaire Estate. An account of Mr. Sinclaire's death in the Corning *Leader* (Corning, N.Y.) that month noted: "Always a lover of beauty, Mr. Sinclaire planted the finest of shrubs, trees and flowers about the spacious ground, thus doing much to beautify the eastern end (of the city) and providing an attractive entrance to the city."

The two story brick structure constituting the former Sinclaire plant was leveled in 1961 to make room for a new shopping center. The beauty of the fine work of this distinguished company will long continue to be admired by glass connoisseurs and collectors everywhere.

SINCLAIRE SIGNED GLASS

Two piece octagon shaped punch bowl height 13", diam. 14". Panels of intaglio cutting alternate with checkerboard motif used in Bird-in-a-cage design. There is a separate panel for strawberry, blackberry, cherry and gooseberry. In the base, the alternate panels are each in a different flower. This is one of Sinclaire's best and rarest designs, probably made on a special order.

Jardiniere, 6¼" tall, 7" diam., chain of hobstars and fan, large clear ovals around the middle. Quality of the glass and cutting the very finest.

Teapot, 9½" from tip of spout to outside rim of handle; hobstar, fan, engraved flowers with curved drape of circles that reduce in size from its center. Over-all effect is one of elegance and charm.

Plate 119

SINCLAIRE INTAGLIO GLASS

Large two piece fruit bowl on a standard in deepest intaglio cut fruit. Bowl is 14½" in diameter, over-all height 14½". Base can be used separately as a compote. Very rare piece of exceptional quality.

Clock, height 10", ornate intaglio cutting of baskets with flowers, cornucopias, etc. over entire front and sides, clock insert by Bailey, Banks & Biddle of Phila., Pa. (original).

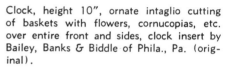

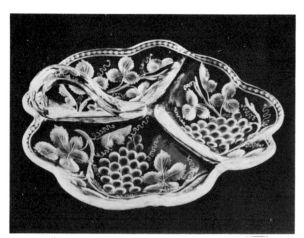

Three sectional dish with applied handle, all cut in Vintage (Intaglio Grape) pattern, note border of elliptical moons around edge.

Plate 120

SIGNED SINCLAIRE GLASS

Vase with two triple notched handles, appr. 12″ tall, 8 arch-shaped panels, alternating hobstars and fan with small flowers.

Card tray, 6¼″ x 7¼″. Fine line cutting around medallion creates very brilliant effect. Outside raised edge is in cross cut diamond.

Pitcher, clear panels marked off by notched vertical lines around top and bottom, chains of hobstars in diamond field. Noteworthy feature is the finely engraved small roses, daisies and small blossoms with fern type leaves. Shape of pitcher is graceful and balanced.

Jardiniere, 6½″ diam. height 7½″, engraved flowers and fern leaves similar to pitcher above.

Plate 121

SIGNED SINCLAIRE GLASS

Large, deep (4") oval bread tray, 14" x 8", intaglio cut flowers and leaves with Russian cutting near the ends, elliptical moon border near rim.

Cone shaped vase 11¼" high, 7½" diam. at top, engraved flowers and leaves, hobstars and fans, with almond shaped ovals and Saint Louis diamond all around.

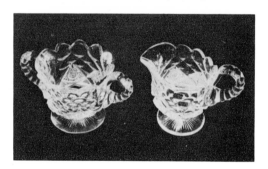

Sugar and creamer on a standard, chain of hobstars in diamond field and Saint Louis diamond motifs.

Unusual variation of vintage pattern with arch shaped panels alternating flower and leaf with brilliant single stars. Tray is 15" x 10½", (collection of Mr. and Mrs. Emerson S. Clavel).

Plate 122

SIGNED SINCLAIRE

Bowl, hexagon shaped with six engraved panels each containing small blossoms and fern leaves, notched lines mark edge of panels, hobstar and notched lines form 1½" chain around bowl.

Bowl, 10" diam., fan between hobstars in a chain, border of engraved leaves with elliptical moons near edge.

Candlesticks, 9¾", intaglio grape pattern cut through emerald green, balance in clear.

Compote, 10" diam. 5¼" high, with chain of hobstars in diamond field, clear flute panels around edge.

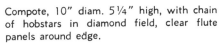

Plate 123

THE STEUBEN GLASS WORKS

The Steuben Glass Works, organized by Thomas G. Hawkes, his son Samuel and Frederick Carder in 1903 became a subsidiary of the Corning Glass Works in 1918.

In the post Brilliant Period, an interest in new kinds of art glass led to the invention, mostly on the initiative of Carder of aurene, rosaline, acid cutback, jade and many other kinds too numerous to specify here. After 1918 and up until just prior to World War II, Steuben did some realistic cutting and made tableware also in cut glass. At the present time most of the ornamental glass being made by Steuben is either without cutting, depending on form (except for the broad facets) or the ornately engraved work of well known artists. In spite of the fact that the prices of some of these objects run into thousands of dollars, this field is more of a "prestige" item than a money-maker for the company.

Pheasant, all over cut in the realistic style (post-Brilliant Period)

Steuben acid cutback covered jar in green with frosted alabaster background, height including knobbed cover approx. 6 inches.

Signed Steuben acid cutback vase in unusual combination of jade green over mandarin yellow, height 6¼". (collection of Leonard J. Pearson)

Plate 124

Plate, 11" diam., pink cut through to alabaster, garlands and wreaths and elliptical "moon" border reminiscent of Sinclaire designs. Most rosaline however was not decorated with cutting.

L. STRAUS & SONS, NEW YORK, N.Y.

The L. Straus & Sons factory (also known as I. Straus & Sons) was a very large cutting house exporting much of their cut glass to Europe. While the quality of and the cutting of the glass was very high, most of the patterns were of standard designs. They did extensive advertising in the *Glass and Crockery Journal* and a few of the patterns given there are here reproduced.

Silver-mounted cut glass bowl.

Plate 125

TIFFANY ART GLASS

Louis Comfort Tiffany (1848-1933), son of the founder of the jewelry firm of Tiffany & Co., New York, N.Y., was one of the great innovator in producing artistic efforts in the use of free form shapes, new colors and combinations of colors and in the texture of his art glass produced first at the Tiffany Glass and Decorating Co. in Corona, L. I., and later by the Tiffany Studios. His production, first started about 1893, continued past the Brilliant Period for cut glass. It is worth while noting that he also did some fine work in intaglio around 1906 similar to designs being used for cut glass. Below are illustrated Tiffany's intaglio grape pattern and a vase with a flower design similar to "Phlox" by Tuthill (see plate 82). The subject of Tiffany glass is, of course, so extensive that we can only mention it here for purposes of comparison.

Pitcher in gold iridescent with pink, lavender and green highlights, cut intaglio grape design, 8½" tall, signed L. C. Tiffany, Favrile. (courtesy of Lillian Nassau)

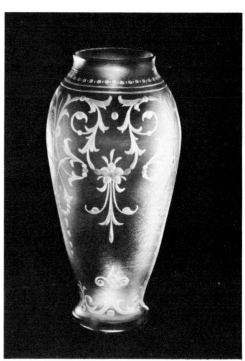

Vase, 8" high in gold iridescent with blue and pink highlights, cut in a design similar to "Phlox" by Tuthill. Note border of "moons" around top rim so common to Sinclaire glass. Vase is signed L. C. Tiffany, Favrile. (courtesy of Lillian Nassau)

Plate 126

TUTHILL CUT GLASS GO. (1900-1923)
Middletown, N.Y.

The Tuthill glass factory was a comparatively small cutting house with an average employment roll of only 30 employees including clerical help. Because of its size, the Tuthill story consists of more than a recital of historical "facts and figures." It is a story of people, personal and intimate, who shared vital common interests, economic and aesthetic. The output of this glass house was a source of great pride to the inhabitants of Middletown and the adjacent areas. One of its great specialties was that exquisite form of embellishment known as "intaglio cut." a deeply carved engraving that results in a three-dimensional effect. The frosty, silvery finish and minutely graduated incisions give it great appeal.

Shortly after starting business, the Tuthill "Grape" pattern won first prize in the St. Louis World's Fair (1904). Though one of many hundreds of plants operating throughout the country, the name of Tuthill was held in such high esteem and its reputation for high quality so unquestioned that it was chosen to create a magnificent dinner service ordered by the Cuban government. It included stemware, pitchers, decanters, plates, cups and saucers, fingerbowls and even bowls for soup. Every single piece bore the engraved coat-of-arms of Cuba.

Another outstanding work designed and cut by Tuthill was a massive and brilliantly decorated vase ordered as a farewell gift for the Chinese ambassador to the United States. The dragon on it "coiled round and round."

A bronze Medal of Honor and Placque was awarded the factory for the finest cut glass exhibited in 1915 at the Panama-Pacific Exposition in San Francisco. Tuthill glass was sold across the nation and abroad at leading department stores and jewelry shops. Corning glass blanks were used.

The family of Tuthill was long prominent in the history of Corning. Henry G. Tuthill, a builder and architect had five sons. One of them, Charles G., had been operating a glass cutting shop in Corning since 1895 when he was 25 years old. He was recognized as a talented craftsman in his field.

Charles opened a small shop in Middletown in 1900. Mr. Ralph "Mike" Salvati, a former employee and "smoother" for the plant, remembers him as about five feet, 11 inches tall and of a quiet and retiring disposition. The work week was 10 hours a day, six days a week. Beginners learning the trade earned about $3.00 a week, the expert engraver $18.00 to $20.00 a week.

Charles met Jennie L. Burt when she came to Middletown from Mountaindale. Her father had been a postmaster there and bored with retirement, opened a small grocery on Little Avenue. Among some of the customers she waited on was Charles. His factory was close by and he came in often. They were soon married.

Susan Crysler of Gouverneur, New York, who had married Charles' brother James F. "The Professor" (superintendent of Middletown schools from 1891 to 1922) came into the business when it was established on 36 Little Avenue about 1903. Susan had been a music instructor for the Middletown schools. She was a fine pianist and generally a very versatile and competent woman.

It was Charles, a man of rare artistic taste and originality who created the designs and ran the workrooms. Susan managed the business end, probably the only woman in the United States to run a cut glass factory. She remained until the factory closed.

On the first floor of the factory were the finished pieces ready to be shipped, freshly washed and glistening, but to be most critically scrutinized by Susan. Tools had to be kept razor sharp to produce a thin hairline mitre cut. She was a rigid perfectionist demanding the utmost in production of quality and in strict adherence to the highest standards. She measured the depth of the cutting, of the scallops and dentil edges. Calipers were used to check on precise alignment of design; everything had to be absolutely perfect.

One of the men responsible for many of the finest pieces and still a resident of Middletown is Harry Holmbraker (later Chief of Police of the town). Unknown generally was the fact that he was one of the outstanding men in the industry in America. Starting when he was only 17 years of age, he studied for seven years to master his art. His equipment consisted of a hundred different copper wheels; one was about the size of a pinhead. He worked for a full year on the Cuban project and engraved the dragon on the gift to the Chinese ambassador previously referred to. Another of his finest and most painstaking works was a vase engraved with tiny birds, each only a quarter-inch high. "Imagine," he said, "the work required on those feathers." He treasures the little dish given to him by Susan in the "Rex" pattern, which won a prize in San Francisco. Another of his precious possessions was a little tumbler with the two inch bust portrait of his wife, surrounded by a feathery fern-like border, which he engraved for her.

Mr. Holmbraker speaks affectionately of Charles and Susan. "The men were inspired. They became enamored with their creations, imbued with the great love of finely engraved brilliant cut glass of flawless beauty, so keenly felt by the Tuthills."

The "Wild Rose" and the "Intaglio Grape" patterns (illustrated elsewhere in this book) were favorites of Charles. Later, in order to compete with the production of pressed and semi-pressed factories, Tuthill tried to steer clear of the "oldtime straightline geometrical patterns and give the public something beyond the reach of the moulded pattern." The engraved and deep cut intaglio designs, framed in brilliant cutting was their attempted solution, a technique that could not be imitated with short-cut cheap methods.

Mr. Brandhurst, an outstanding polisher and engraver, had worked for O'Connor while he had been manager of the Dorflinger works. He had also been employed by the Imperial Glass Company of Philadelphia, L. Straus, Unger Brothers and many others. When he came to Middletown in 1904 and asked to see the superintendent at the Tuthill factory, he was surprised when a lady (Susan Tuthill) appeared. "We know that the standards of the cut glass business are being lowered," she said. "Inferior glass and half-pressed glass seem to satisfy many of the public, but we will never compromise. I want the most capable craftsmen working for me and I'd like to have you join us." Mr. Brandhurst did join them, and remained until the very end. His starting salary, about as high as they paid anywhere, was $18.00 a week for a six day week, "and no coffee-breaks. If you come one minute late you were called on the carpet. She ran it sort of like a school, very strictly" he reminisced.

Some of the men responsible for the intricately cut and engraved work are still living in Middletown. Unfortunately, the era of this glass factory coincided with the decline in interest and markets for the product. The Tuthill factory, maintaining its high standards to the end, was finally forced to stop production. Susan Tuthill settled in California after the factory closed. The stock, blanks, equipment, patterns and photographs were eventually sold to Henry Gogard Co. of Honesdale.

Recently, several examples of Tuthill glass were presented by members of the Tuthill family to the Los Angeles Museum which had requested it for its glass collection.

Mediocrity in Tuthill production is conspicuously absent. Tuthill patterns are brilliantly conceived and expertly executed on the finest Corning blanks made at the time. Practically any piece of Tuthill is a choice collector's item. Unfortunately, the output of this outstanding company was comparatively limited.

TUTHILL SIGNED GLASS

Jardiniere in "Wild Rose" design with vesicas in small sharp relief diamond, height 6⅛", 7¾" in diameter.

Vase in very fine example of Tuthill's "intaglio grape" pattern, 19 inches tall.

Two piece punch bowl, 13¾" in diam. with height the same, has 6 point star with sharp hobnail and beading, very sharp cross hatched bands and Russian cutting. Also hobstars, strawberry diamond and fan motifs. Circa 1915, it was once owned by former Mayor Cox of Middletown.

Plate 127

TUTHILL INTAGLIO GLASS

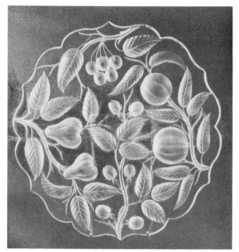

Flat tray 12¼" diameter. The depth of the cutting and the shading make this an exceptionally fine example of Tuthill's intaglio.

Pitcher 8⅝" tall with large intaglio cut flowers.

Sugar and creamer on a standard in deep intaglio. Note elegant and unique shape.

Plate 128

TUTHILL INTAGLIO GLASS

Basket, 14" tall including handle, unsigned but typical of Tuthill combination of geometric motifs with intaglio cutting and identified as Tuthill by Ralph Salvati, formerly "smoother" for that company.

Pickle dish, 4¼" x 6¾", 2" deep, chain of hobstars and intaglio flower motifs.

Shallow bowl, 10" in diameter. Fine line cutting similar to bowl at left.

8" bowl. Note fine lines and detail.

Plate 129

TUTHILL SIGNED GLASS

Cakestand on a low standard, 12" in diameter, note unusual 24 point hobstar center with fans between the points.

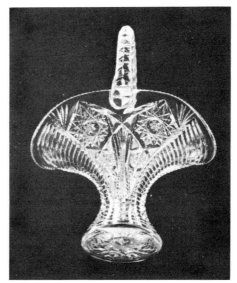

Basket, 10½" high including handle, horizontal step cutting motif used with brilliant effect.

Carafe, 8" tall, similar to design of cakestand (upper left) with parallel line cutting added, single star base.

Two exquisitely cut 7" plates in original, unique Tuthill designs.

Plate 130

TUTHILL CUT GLASS

Tall vase with large, wide ribbed handles, unsigned, (collection of Mrs. Frank Powell Tuthill).

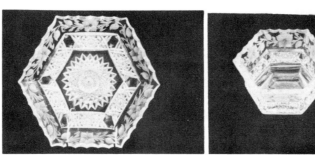

Mayonnaise plate (6¼"), and dish, set (signed).

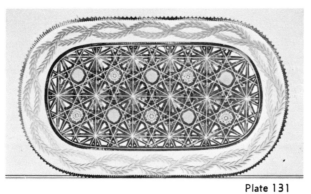

Rectangular shaped tray, 6" x 10" in variation of Russian design, raised edge engraved with double chain of leaves, (signed).

Plate 131

CAMEO GLASS—AMERICAN, FRENCH AND ENGLISH

In his book *19th Century British Glass*, Hugh Wakefield writes that the Brilliant Period is a "term which may reasonably be extended to the equivalent phase in Britain and elsewhere . . ." About 1895 E. Hammond was decorating bowls for Stevens & Williams in what looks like the American motifs of cane, pillar and Russian. A cookie jar in the possession of the author is in Russian cutting and signed "Edinburgh, Scotland."

In 1880 Thomas Webb & Sons in England was making "rock crystal" in floral patterns with birds and other objects in deep engraving brilliantly polished and very similar to the Hawkes "rock crystal". Its production of it continued throughout the 1890's.

In the 1880's, cameo glass was being made in England on a commercial basis by Thomas Webb & Sons and other firms. In 1889 Galle was exhibiting cameo glass in Paris, France, in new motifs of flowers, leaves and insects, obviously influenced by his familiarity with Japanese art. Galle, an active participant in the Art Nouveau movement, received wide attention for his originality of colors and forms in his acid etched and engraved work with cased glass. Some examples of cameo or "cameo type" glass are here illustrated.

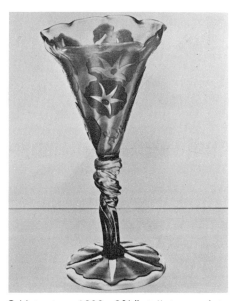

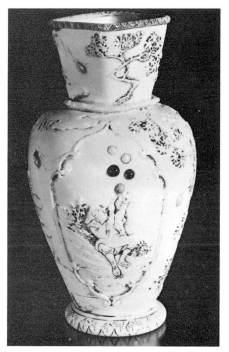

Goblet, circa 1890, 8⅜" tall in an Art Nouveau "free form," has a mauve foot with radiating ribs, bowl is in blue with frosted gray radiants from a green twisted stem. Similar to one in **Journal of Glass Studies**, Vol. 5, 1963 on page 107 fig. 3 (published by the Corning Museum of Glass).

Vase, 7¾" tall with square top, ivory colored, signed "Webb," a rare piece of cameo circa 1880-1885, carved mainly by hand tools. Has jewel inserts.

Plate 132

Basket, cameo, 8" square with deeply fluted top, made by the Mt. Washington Glass Co. The outer layer of pink overlay is cut through to white with griffins and floral sprays in relief. This is similar to one on exhibit at the Corning Museum of Glass.

In Greek mythology, Perseus slew Medusa, one of the snaky haired sisters whose horrible aspect turned the beholder to stone. The above perfume bottle with the carved head of Medusa on the front in green stands out in relief from a background of a dark dusty pink. On the back of this ovoid shaped bottle is the winged helmet of Perseus with a dagger through it. Snakes are also carved on each side and there is a snake entwined around the stopper with his head raised. This magnificent piece is the work of E. Michel (signed), the finest engraver of glass in France of his period.

Plate 133

RARITIES IN CUT GLASS

Gone-with-the-wind oil lamp in three pieces, consisting of a base, the font and top globe, over-all height 29 inches, every bit cut in hobstar, pinwheel, hobnail, strawberry diamond, **cane** and fan, with border of clear flutes near the base. This brilliant, rare piece is an object considered by many characteristic of the mid-Victorian period.

Plate 134

RARITIES

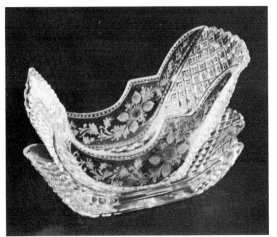

Sled (in two sections) cross cut diamond with sides of upper section engraved with flowers and leaves.

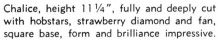

Chalice, height 11¼", fully and deeply cut with hobstars, strawberry diamond and fan, square base, form and brilliance impressive.

Chalice on long knobbed teardrop stem, 16" tall, elegant form combined with sharp brilliance. Note detailed cutting of base.

Coffee pot with cover, in "Florence" pattern, thumbprint notched spout and handle.

Plate 135

Huge chalice punch bowl, specially made, 10″ in diameter, height 15″, with 12 matching punch cups. Center hobstar with notched radiants is encircled with chain of hobstars. Fully and sharply cut, very brilliant.

Champagne ice bucket has silver plated liner. In variation of the "Florence" pattern. Height 11″, diameter 9″.

Ice bucket or jardiniere, height 9″, 8″ in diam. Chain of hobstars near top and bottom and panels with single stars frame large intaglio cut pictures of roses and leaves. Top rim border in vintage design.

Plate 136

RARITIES

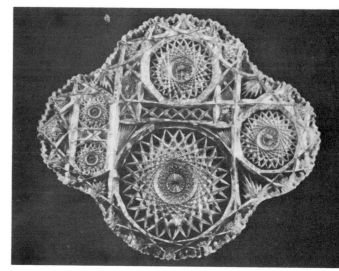

Dresser tray with depressions for placing perfume bottles, powder box and rectangular shaped patch box, 10" x 11½".

Chalice type vase, approx. 16" high with large pinwheel, hobstar, strawberry diamond and notched prism. Base cut in notched prism radiants.

Cake stand, 10" diam. 9¼" high, in chain of hobstars motif with a 1½" gallery cut all around with single stars.

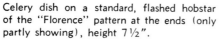

Celery dish on a standard, flashed hobstar of the "Florence" pattern at the ends (only partly showing), height 7½".

Plate 137

RARITIES

Cornucopia, 12½″ x 6″ wide, on a standard, in hobstar, strawberry diamond and cross cut diamond, quality of glass and cutting exceptional.

Pair of unusual, brilliantly cut compotes with tops that flare out and are fluted, knobbed teardrop stems and fully cut bases. The prism motif around the irregular edge enhances the sparkling over-all effect. Approximate height, 8 inches.

Plate 138

RARITIES

Eperne, top screws into center, overall height 25 inches, lower section 8½" high, 12" in diameter, cut in hobstar, strawberry diamond, cane and clear flute.

Sugar and creamer on a high standard with knobbed teardrop stems, approx. height 6". It is easy to understand why this is one of the most sought after items in American cut glass.

Plate 139

RARITIES

Left:
Vase, 24" tall, fully cut with vertical columns of hobstars that alternate with columns of notched prism; sunbursts and stars above beading near top and below beading near base.

Right: Large jug, 15" tall, 6" diam., cut in basketweave pattern.

Vase in unusual shape, 11⅞" tall with 7" spread at top, horizontal step cutting on sides, stem is in Saint Louis (concave) diamond.

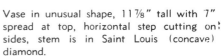

Vase, uniquely placed on three clear legs, 11½" tall, cut in hobstar and Harvard pattern.

Plate 140

BASKETS

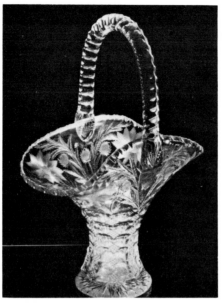

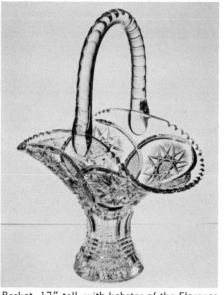

Basket, 14" x 9½", with intaglio cut flowers.

Basket, 17" tall, with hobstar of the Florence pattern and hobnail vesicas.

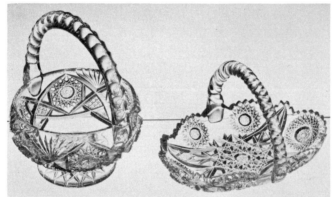

Left: basket on a standard, 8" tall x 5¼" in diam. Right: low basket, the dish itself 8½" x 5½", in "Expanding Star" pattern, with triple notched handle.

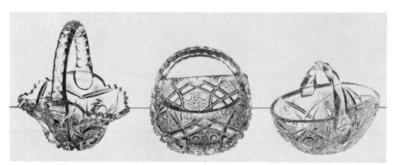

Small baskets: (left to right) A. 5½" tall in pinwheel and cane, signed "Clark"; B. Nut basket 5" tall, hobstars, fan and cane with clear split bands; C. Basket in Dorflinger's Middlesex pattern, with twisted handle.

Plate 141

BOTTLES

Bottle with hinged sterling stopper that turns and locks.

Cordial bottle signed Hawkes in "rock crystal."

Medicine bottle for water with hollow stopper for pills, etc.

Worcestershire sauce in Venetian pattern.

Ketchup bottle, 7½" high including stopper.

Bitters bottle.

Perfume in Russian pattern with sterling screw top.

Perfume in Chrysanthemum with sterling overlay stopper.

Plate 142

BOWLS

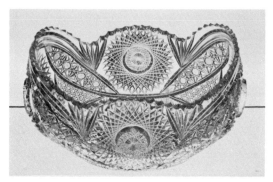

Orange bowl, 10½" x 7", with 32 point hobstars, fan and cane.

Banana bowl on a standard.

Banana bowl, in irregular shape, scalloped, serrated edge, 13½" x 8¾".

Orange bowl on standard in cane with hobstars in a circle of clear, ridged edge, bowl 6" x 9½".

Large bowl with two sides that turn in, 10¾" x 8", chain of hobstars and prism motifs, 48 point hobstar base.

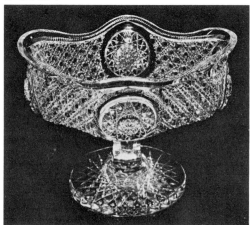

Plate 143

BOXES

Large hinged jewel box, 6" x 9½".

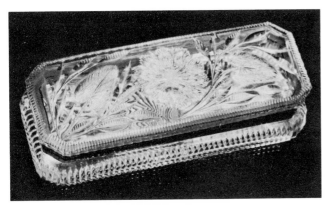

Glove box, 10¾" x 4", top cut in intaglio flowers and leaves, top and bottom edges in vertical prism.

Hinged powder box, top and front view, 5" diam. at top, 6½" at bottom, 5" high.

Plate 144

CABINET PIECES

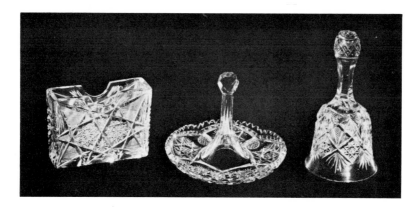

Top row (left to right) : A. Holder for deck of cards; B. Stick dish with Florence hobstar and hobnail vesica; C. Bell in Dorflinger's Middlesex pattern.
Middle row: D. Toothpick holder in unusual shape; E. Mustard jar with sterling top and handle; F. Toothpick holder on a standard; G. Paste jar with sterling top and on handle of the brush.
Bottom row: H. Fairy lamp with three wide ridged openings in the center of large hobstars, also vesicas in strawberry diamond; I. Nut dish in "Open Petal" pattern of Louis Hinsberger, patent number 39313.

Plate 145

CABINET PIECES

Top row (left to right): A. Bell with "X" cut vesica, hobstar and fan; B. Large bell, height 7½"; C. Bell with flashed star in a diamond field.

Middle row: D. Compote with air twist stem, signed "Clark"; E. canoe; F. Bitters bottle with sterling topped stopper, in hobnail pattern, signed Hawkes.

Bottom row: G. Plate 8" diam. and goblet, 7" tall, with border of engraved flowers cut through blue to clear, rest of plate and goblet in clear, signed Hawkes (collection of Martin J. Desmoni).

Plate 146

CABINET PIECES

Top row (left to right) : A. Handled mug; B. Inkwell with matching lid, cut in hobstar, bullseye and fan, signed Hawkes; C. Sugar shaker in Greek Key.
Middle row: D. Spooner vase in "Pinetree" pattern; E. Lemonade in Greek Key; F. Carafe in Louis XIV.
Bottom row: G. Small butter dish, dome only 4" diam.; H. Smelling salts jar in Harvard pattern; I. Cup and saucer with unusual 6 point center star and rosettes between the points (collection of Mr. & Mrs. Richard Karaus).

Plate 147

CABINET PIECES

Handled mayonnaise bowl and tray; wine washer, chain of hobstars and honeycomb (concave diamond) motifs, 4½" by 6", signed Sinclaire.

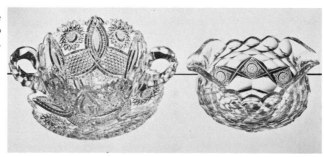

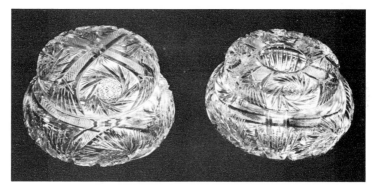

Toothpick on a standard in Harvard with details of motif enlarged.

Dresser set consisting of powder box and hair receiver in pinwheel and bars of strawberry diamond motifs.

Covered mustard jar and syrup pitcher in Venetian pattern, syrup has sterling top and handle.

Flat paperweight candleholders in Dorflinger's Middlesex pattern.

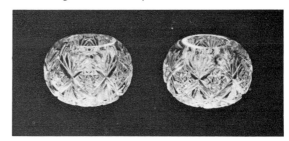

Plate 148

CANDLESTICKS

Unusual shape, height 12", combines geometric motifs with intaglio cut flowers and leaves.

Chain of hobstars in diamond field and flute motifs, teardrop stem, 12" tall, 24 point hobstar base.

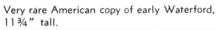

Very rare American copy of early Waterford, 11¾" tall.

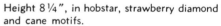

Height 8¼", in hobstar, strawberry diamond and cane motifs.

Plate 149

CANDLESTICKS—CONSOLE SET

Console set in "Old Colony" pattern (reproduced from a catalogue of the Pairpoint Corporation.)

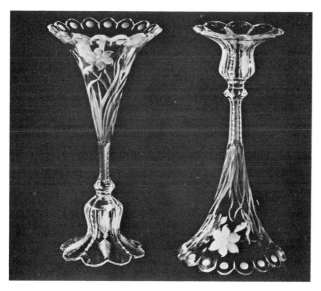

Pair of candlesticks, reversible for use as vases if desired, 9" tall, engraved feather and flowers with ribbon type leaves, hollow open bottoms, border of moons near base, unsigned but probably Sinclaire.

Plate 150

AMERICAN COLORED CUT GLASS

Left to right: Signed Libbey candlestick in sapphire blue, teardrop stem, 12" tall in panel cut with deeply ridged radiants in base; Bread tray in ruby red, 14" x 7", cut to clear in hobstar strawberry diamond and fan; Libbey candlestick (signed) in emerald green, upper side of base intaglio cut to an unpolished gray with flowers and leaves.

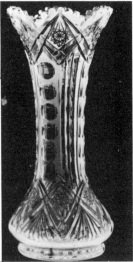

Left to right: Signed Hawkes compote in ruby red, inside of bowl (6¾") has 1½" border of engraved flowers and leaves; Rosebowl in sapphire blue, 4¾" diam. in hobstar cross cut diamond, cane and fan motifs; Vase in amethyst 12½" tall, chain of hobstars, prism and bullseye motifs.

Plate 151

AMERICAN COLORED CUT GLASS

Left to right: Signed Libbey compote in emerald green, 6 inch bowl has clear panels, the flowers and leaves on bowl and upper part of base are intaglio cut to frosted gray; Signed Hawkes covered candy dish on a standard in turquoise, 5¾" tall, Millicent pattern; Cruet, emerald green in panel cut to clear, height 9⅝", single star base.

Banana dish, 10¾" long by 5" wide, cut from cranberry red to clear, sides turn in toward center, strawberry diamond, star and fan pattern, (rare).

Plate 152

CRUETS AND DECANTERS

Left to right:
Triangle shaped cruet, signed Hawkes in hobstar, cross-cut diamond and fan; Cruet, 8¼" tall including stopper, in bullseye, strawberry diamond and star; Cruet on a standard, panel cut neck, in Hawkes (signed) Middlesex pattern.

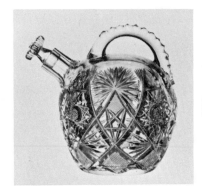

Jug, height 7" to top of triple-notched handle, hobstar and flashed fan motifs.

Left to right:
Cruet signed Clark, base has strawberry diamond and fan radiants; Cruet signed Libbey, height 6⅝" including stopper; Cruet with hobnail in diamond shaped field, notched prism and strawberry diamond motifs, sterling overlay stopper.

Shot glass and matching decanter in flat ovoid shape, 9⅛" to top of stopper, ring handle, 24 point hobstar with sharp, deeply cut notched prism at the sides.

Plate 153

DECANTERS

Pair of decanters, height 12½" including original matching teardrop stoppers, base cut in strawberry diamond and fan radiants.

Decanter 15" tall including original matching stopper. Work comparable to finest of Joseph Locke. Acid etched and engraved delicate small blossoms and large leaves with superb nuances in the unpolished surfaces.

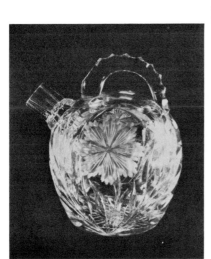

Left to right: Jug with notched handle over top, intaglio cut flower; Tall small necked decanter with low notched handle, height including stopper 14 inches; Square decanter with handle from corner edge, 10" tall, in hobstar and prism.

Plate 154

GOBLETS

A. Unusual shape in Russian and fan, teardrop stem, ridged radiants; B. Chain of hobstars and fan, clear panels where bowl narrows, signed Hawkes; C. Unusual knobbed teardrop at bottom of stem, signed Libbey.

D. Hawkes Gravic, intaglio cut iris; E. Chains of hobstars, bands of strawberry diamond and cane, double teardrop stem; F. Goblet in fine line cutting, height 7¾″, in Millicent pattern, signed Hawkes, (collection of Mr. and Mrs. Richard Karaus).

G. Rhine wine, 7″ tall, bowl in emerald green cut to clear, knobbed teardrop stem, pattern by L. Straus & Sons; H. Princess pattern, diamond cut knobbed stem, signed Libbey; I. Goblet in same pattern as G. (Rhine wine) but in clear, signed with L. Straus and Sons trademark of star in circle

Plate 155

JARS, COOKIE, CANDY, SACHET, ETC.

A. Cookie jar 8½" tall including diamond cut finial, in Brunswick pattern (with fan included);
B. Candy jar, 7" high, 4" diameter; C. Tobacco jar 7½" high in J. Hoare variation of Creswick.

D. Sachet jar with sterling rim and hinged cover, has separate inside glass stopper; E. Caviar jar with inner glass liner and matching tray, deeply cut in hobstar, strawberry diamond and fan, 7" high including knobbed cover; F. Sachet jar, hinged sterling cover (monogrammed) in variation of Middlesex pattern, separate inside stopper, 5" high.

Plate 156

KNIFE RESTS

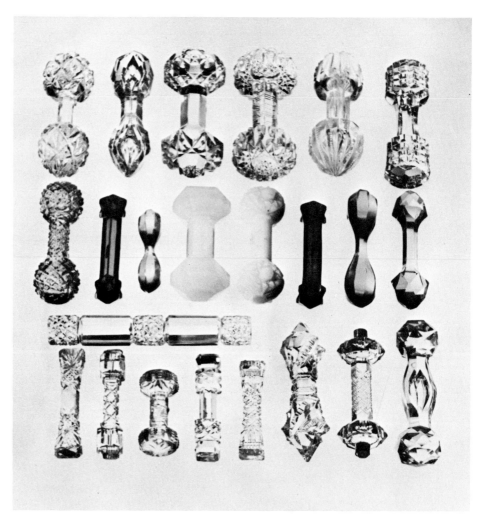

Collection of knife rests: Top row, 2nd and 5th from left have teardrops in each end; Second row, colored knife rests: (a) pink rose, (b) amethyst, (c) turquoise, (d) and (e) milk glass, (f) cobalt blue, (g) amber and (h) turquoise. Between 2nd and 3rd rows, the double knife rest is for a carving set. Bottom row: 6th from left has notched swirl ends, 7th has sterling covered ends, 8th has teardrop in center bar.

Plate 157

LAMPS

Lamp, height 22″, dome approximately 12″ in diameter, Intaglio Grape (identical in detail to signed Tuthill) on one side (upper left), and intaglio cut berries on the other side (upper right), with the rest in Harvard.

Lamp 23″ tall, with mushroom shaped dome 13½″ in diameter, every bit cut in sharp Harvard with horizontal step cutting around the center of the stem of the base.

Plate 158

LAMPS

Left: Lamp approximately 21″ tall, dome 12″ diameter, wide panels of deeply cut notched prism alternating with hobstar in a hexagon and strawberry diamond, very brilliant; Right: Lamp, 23″ tall, shade 12″ diameter, hobstar, strawberry diamond, hobnail and band radiants of single stars.

Lamp, height 23″, dome 12″ diameter, in hobstar, strawberry diamond and fan with beautifully designed base having the added motifs of clear panel and honeycomb (concave diamond).

Plate 159

MINIATURES AND WHIMSIES

Row 1 (top row): Gone-with-the-wind lamp in emerald green cut to clear, sterling base; Book, used as a paperweight; Pitcher, salesman's sample.
Row 2: Salesman's sample dish, 2¾" x 4¼"; Salt dish in Russian pattern; Book, 2" x 2½"; Ashtray.
Row 3: Salesman's samples of handled nappy, ice bucket and two other nappies.
Row 4: Cigar holder in cranberry red cut to clear; Seal; Book, only ¾" x 9/16"; Heart.

Plate 160

NAPKIN RINGS

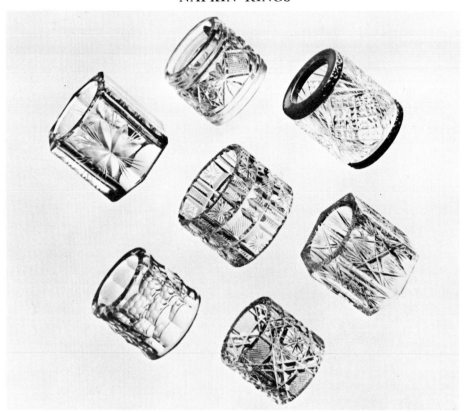

Top row (looking diagonally from higher to lower): Chain of hobstars alternating with strawberry diamond, also fan motif; Cross cut diamond and fan, rimmed with sterling silver. Row 2: Intaglio cut star and fan; Strawberry diamond and star pattern; Hobstars, fan and single stars. Row 3: Saint Louis (concave) diamond; Harvard pattern.

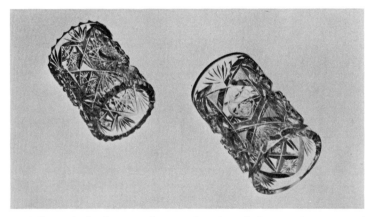

Napkin rings specially made for large napkins used at formal dinners, the one on the right has been monogrammed.

PLATE 161

PITCHERS

Very tall tankard pitcher, height 18″, chain of hobstars at top, vertical panels with bulls-eyes alternate with columns of notched prism.

Large wide pitcher on a standard, intaglio cut Butterfly pattern with background of flowers and leaves, 10″ tall.

Pitcher 11½″ tall, ·with vertical columns of cane variation, feather and beading motifs, base has four strawberry diamond squares with clear circles in their centers.

PLATE 162

PITCHERS

Left: Pitcher 12½" tall in Greek Key pattern with wide sterling top and lip.
Right: Pitcher on a standard, 11½" high, rare and exquisite form, cut in hobstars, strawberry diamond, bands of cane and fan.

Syrup pitcher, 6¾"; Milk pitcher 4"; Squat cider pitcher 6¾" tall, signed Libbey, with typical spread fan figure in notched prism.

Barrel shaped pitcher, 7" high and matching plate 7½" in diameter in Russian (star button) pattern.

PLATE 163

STEMWARE

Illustrated below is a variation of the "X" Split Vesica pattern (plate 32), similar to Straus pattern patent 24202. The vesica, however, is in hobstar and strawberry diamond instead of cane and stars. Note that all of the stemware have double teardrop stems. Bases are stippled with cross hatched strawberry diamond.

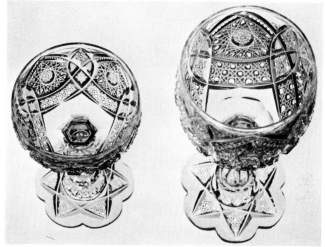

Top view of supreme (left) and goblet to show design.

Left to right: Shot glass, juice, liqueur and sherry.

Left to right: Water goblet; large (red wine) claret; wine, (white wine) and champagne glass.

PLATE 164

STEMWARE AND CENTER HANDLE DISHES

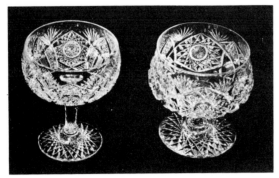

Supremes: (left) 4⅝" diameter 5¼" high; (right) "X" cut vesica, hobstar and fan motifs, 4¾" high.

Parfait, chain of hobstars and strawberry diamond, balance in notched prism; Jelly dish on standard, teardrop stem; Parfait 6½" tall in Parisian pattern.

Center handle dish, 10" diameter, chain of hobstars enclose cut flowers and leaves, signed "Hunt".

Stick bonbon dish, 8" high, hobstars and notched prism, single star knob (rare); (at right): Stick dish with question mark handle on heart shaped dish (??)

Left to right: Wine glass, 4¾" and cocktail glass 4⅛" tall, with knobbed teardrop stems, strawberry diamond hexagons around a star ("cluster"), cane and blaze.

PLATE 165

SUGAR AND CREAMER SETS

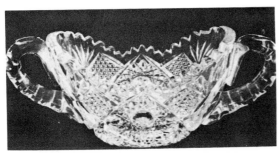

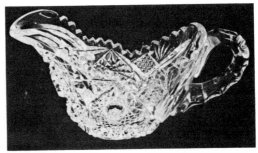

Set, unusual wide shape, sugar 7⅝", creamer 6¾" (including handles), in hobstar, hobnail and fan motifs.

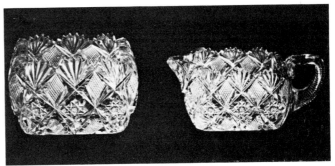

Covered sugar (5½" to top of diamond cut knob), creamer, on legs, in hobstar, strawberry diamond and hobnail.

Square shaped sugar (4") and creamer, hobstar, strawberry diamond and fan, hobstar base.

Sugar (4" tall) and creamer on a standard, in Harvard pattern.

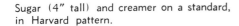

PLATE 166

TRAYS

Round tray, 12" in diameter, in Flutes and Hobstar pattern (see Plate 89).

12" tray, of unusual shape and design with "shell" scallops of notched fans that are flashed at the ends with fine line cutting.

Tray 16½" x 9½" with two "fishtail" ends, in unique design.

Oval tray, 14" x 8". Triple lines of beading, strawberry diamond and cane enclose a center hobstar that is filled in with small hobnail motif.

PLATE 167

TUMBLERS

Left to right: tumblers (a) Hobstar, strawberry diamond and fan, paperweight bottom; (b) Wheat pattern by Tuthill (signed), paperweight bottom; (c) Deep intaglio cut tiger lily, 3¾" high; (d) Chain of hobstars and fans, swirled flutes and notching, signed Hawkes.

Highball tumblers (a) 5½" tall; (b) Thistle pattern with triple line cutting variation of cane, 4¾" tall; (c) Vertical band of stars, hobstar, strawberry diamond and fan, 5" tall.

VASES

Left: One of a pair of bud vases with paperweight bottoms, 7½" high, unsigned but looks like the work of Sinclaire or Tuthill.

Right: Vase 14" tall, chain of hobstars and fans, with five panels formed by notched lines, each containing engraved daisies with fern type leaves, signed Sinclaire.

PLATE 168

VASES

Vase in unusual shape and design, bulbous at bottom, narrows with slight bulge in middle, then flares out at top, bands of hobnail and cane, hobstars, honeycomb, stars and horizontal step cutting.

Height 10", upper half deeply engraved with birds, leaves and flowers, balance in geometric patterns of cane, strawberry diamond and fan, signed "N.C.G."

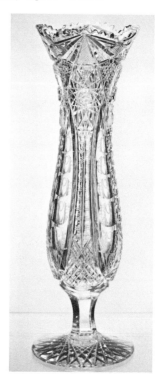

Left: Vase 18" tall, long fluted panels with hobstar chains top and middle, bulbous part in hobstar, strawberry diamond, bullseye, fan and single star, signed Hawkes.

Right: Footed vase 18" tall, bullseyes, hobstars, cross cut diamond and beading.

PLATE 169

TRADEMARKS

J. D. Bergen
Meriden, Conn.

T. B. Clark & Co., Inc.
Honesdale, Pa.

C. Dorflinger & Sons, Inc.
White Mills, Pa.

O. F. Egginton Co.
Corning, New York

H. C. Fry Glass Co.
Rochester, Pa.

T. G. Hawkes & Co.
Corning, New York

J. Hoare & Co.
Corning, N. Y.

The Libbey Glass Mfg. Co.
Toledo, Ohio

Maple City Glass Co.
Taken over by—
T. B. Clark Co.
Honesdale, Pa.

Mount Washington Glass Co.
South Boston, Mass.
(Sometime between 1894-1896
became part of Pairpoint Corp.)

Pairpoint Corp.
New Bedford, Mass.

Quaker City Cut Glass Co.
Philadelphia, Pa.

SINCLAIRE

H. P. Sinclaire & Co.
Corning, N. Y.

L. Straus & Sons*
also known as
I. Straus & Sons
New York, N. Y.

Tuthill Cut Glass Co.
Middletown, N. Y.

Special Note:
The acid etched star within a circle was used only on Straus Patents and appears to be their modification of the Straus Trademark (above). It is interesting to observe that the star within a circle was a trademark registered by the Libbey Glass Co., April 16, 1901 but was never as far as we know used to mark their cut and engraved glass.